The SuperQuack

Stories of Healing from *Out of Left Field*

Hoberleigh Phreigh

BALBOA.
PRESS
A DIVISION OF HAY HOUSE

Balboa Press books may be ordered through booksellers or by contacting:

Balboa Press
A Division of Hay House
1663 Liberty Drive
Bloomington, IN 47403
www.balboapress.com
1-(877) 407-4847

Because of the dynamic nature of the Internet, any web addresses or links contained in this book may have changed since publication and may no longer be valid. The views expressed in this work are solely those of the author and do not necessarily reflect the views of the publisher, and the publisher hereby disclaims any responsibility for them.

The author of this book does not dispense medical advice or prescribe the use of any technique as a form of treatment for physical, emotional, or medical problems without the advice of a physician, either directly or indirectly. The intent of the author is only to offer information of a general nature to help you in your quest for emotional and spiritual well-being. In the event you use any of the information in this book for yourself, which is your constitutional right, the author and the publisher assume no responsibility for your actions.

Duck graphic used on interior by Brandy Doll

Printed in the United States of America.

ISBN: 978-1-4525-8119-4 (sc)
ISBN: 978-1-4525-8121-7 (hc)
ISBN: 978-1-4525-8120-0 (e)

Library of Congress Control Number: 2013915655

Balboa Press rev. date: 11/07/2013

This book is dedicated to all the open-minded readers who are willing to consider the possibility that energetic techniques can heal mind, body, and spirit. May you find something in these pages that will assist you in your own journey of exploration beyond the physical realm.

Table of Contents

Note to the Reader

I have included a glossary at the end of this book. When a word or term is followed by an asterisk (*), you will find a brief definition and/or a website link to assist with clarification.

Foreword

If the title of this book caused you to grin and chuckle into your sleeve, I have a feeling that the subtitle might have made you roll your eyes and perhaps even elicited a groan. Maybe you are saying, "Is this writer serious? *Stories of Healing from Out of Left Field?* Is this supposed to inspire confidence?" The term "out of left field" comes from baseball, and although people dispute the origin of its use as a slang term, it has come to mean an action or event that is strange, odd, or unexpected. A friend of mine who is a baseball fan once explained that when a left fielder throws a ball toward home plate, the runner from third is surprised as the ball whizzes past him. So with regard to the subtitle, think of the word *unexpected*.

Let's imagine for a moment that right field represents the ordinary, everyday world perceivable by the five senses (and instruments, such as telescopes and microscopes, that enhance those senses). As this idiomatic expression suggests, we are in a cultural climate that is oriented in this direction. And when we look in this direction, we see the objective and interobjective world. This is the world that empirical science studies.

Left field is the world of ideas, feelings, emotions, and the cultural climate itself. They are real things and events, but we do not access them through the senses. You will never look in a microscope and see love, compassion, justice, art, literature, or poetry on the slide. Yet we experience all of those things just as surely as the objective world. Left field represents, therefore, the subjective and intersubjective world. People study and express it through endeavors such as the arts, religion, introspective psychology, and philosophy. Is left field sounding a bit more comfortable now?

Let's carry the analogy a bit further. In order to have the baseball game we are familiar with, we need both left and right field. To eliminate either would diminish the interest and symmetry of the game. It would also effectively eliminate center field, and center field is an ideal place to get a good view of both.

Notice that the farther out from the viewer in either field you go, the more subtle the perspective from home plate. Imagine that the subtleness of right field would be the domain of, for example, subatomic physics. Subatomic particles are much more difficult to perceive and might even seem a bit mysterious, as any reading about quantum mechanics will demonstrate, but *we are still in right field.* Conversely, the farther you go out into left field, the more subtle those interior occasions become, and as subjective left-field events, they look extremely mystical and are often interpreted as spiritual. A rational worldview often finds them bizarre and difficult to believe. But keep in mind that we cannot see everything in the left field with the physical senses.

This book is the story of one person's journey of exploration into the farther reaches of left field, based on her interior lived experience and years of spiritual practice. At times, she seems like the runner from third to home who is surprised by that ball thrown from left field, but as her awareness has grown, she has come to expect the unexpected and to use it in her life and healing energy work. She does not attempt to convince the closed-minded cynic, but she does invite the open-minded skeptic to share her experiences and perhaps to even further his or her own explorations.

Teri D'Andria, BA, MSOM, DAOM

Preface

I am not a writer. Until recently, I never considered writing a book. The reason this book came to be is twofold: first, to let people know that energy work is real and, second, to help others having out-of-left-field experiences know they are not alone.

Energy healing techniques not only work but also can be life changing. My interest stems from my own journey of experiencing various forms of emotional and physical discomfort and seeking out ways to heal myself when the accepted Western methods didn't give me the results I hoped for. I have been introduced to many energetic techniques that have worked well for me, and I've been able to use these techniques to help others.

All of the stories in these pages are presented as accurately as I can recall, and I've done my best to make recent confirmations with others involved to ensure my accuracy as well as to establish the long-term validity of my work.

Whereas much of the book describes healing work, there is much more to this plane of existence than what we experience with our senses, so I have included a few stories of other anomalous phenomena in order to demonstrate that point. These include such experiences as being out of my body and traveling to another realm beyond the physical, visiting my mother after her death, recalling my twin's death while still in the womb, and hearing nonphysical entities speak to me. I also have included mechanisms and philosophies that have helped me in my personal journey in life and I've given examples how others have been helped, as well, with the intention of revealing how energy healing can be effective.

I have questioned my sanity more than a time or two during these unusual experiences, and I have been comforted by others who have shared their own experiences with me. That has led to understanding, healing, and a greater sense of enlightenment. If sharing my stories can do that for others who are faced with similar issues, then I am willing to look foolish to nonbelievers. I believe my journey has helped me grow not only as a human being but also as a spiritual being.

Why I Call Myself
the Super*Quack*

Why would an honest, self-respecting practitioner of energy healing call herself a superquack? Do I really consider myself a quack? Well, no. However, there are quite a number of people who consider the work of energy healing to be quackery, and at one time, I was one of them. After years of extensive study and success in my practice, I have changed my mind. While I do take my work seriously, I don't take myself seriously. On that score, I am willing to use humor to get my point across. This book is the story of my journey from a cold skeptic to a curious explorer to a believer with such passion that I have made energy healing my life's work.

My qualifications run the gamut of degree programs, course series, and workshops, spanning over twenty-five years.

Here is an outline of my training and background:

In 1985, I became interested in healing techniques and received my first Reiki attunements,* eventually becoming a Reiki master.

In 1987, I began studying Science of Mind* and became a licensed Religious Science practitioner.*

In 1999, I graduated with my master's degree from Samra University of Oriental Medicine and became a licensed acupuncturist.

Since that time, I have studied various modalities, including the following:

Touch for Health
Nambudripad's Allergy Elimination Technique (NAET)*
Jaffee Mellor Technique (JMT)*
Neuro-Emotional Technique (NET)*
BodyTalk*
Emotional Freedom Techniques (EFT)*
Matrix Energetics*
Reconnective Healing
Quantum Touch*
ThetaHealing*
Genome Healing*
Pranic Healing*

I have put together my own modality, incorporating many of the techniques listed above, to quickly—and often permanently—release the emotional impact of past traumas.

The training of a superquack was a serious commitment, as my friends would happily attest each and every time I announced the pursuit of another healing technique. In fact, a well-meaning, supportive friend dubbed me a superquack when I shared with her the description of another class I was going to take.

"What are you going to call yourself once you get certified in this new technique?" she asked.

"Well," I answered, "all I can tell you is that from the course description, it sounds like I will be able to do everything but walk on water once I complete it. It sounds so unbelievable that I think I'm going to have to call myself a quack."

Her grin turned to laughter as she said with all sincerity, "I think you are going to be a superquack."

I have learned to not be offended by the term *quack* when it is applied to me. I have, in fact, been called a quack to my face. I don't take it personally, because the few people who have said it were unfamiliar with my work. If indeed I am a quack, so be it. But I am one confident quack who gets results.

With a name like *The SuperQuack*, you've probably guessed that this book is not going to be a scientific tome of how energy works. If you are curious as to some of the evidence and research that exists, I suggest you seek out the writings of Dr. Candace Pert, who wrote *Molecules of Emotion: The Science Behind Mind-Body Medicine*. Read Gregg Braden, a *New York Times* best-selling author who is well known in both the world of science and the world of spirituality. His books include *The God Code*, *The Divine Matrix*, *Fractal Time*, and *Deep Truth*. Or read any of Dr. Bruce Lipton's books. I recommend *The Biology of Belief: Unleashing the Power of Consciousness, Matter & Miracles* and *The Wisdom of Your Cells: How Your Beliefs Control Your Biology*. These are only three of the many brilliant minds proving the scientific reality behind what once was considered quackery. While I share my experiences, they offer scientific evidence.

All of the stories you are about to read are real events culled from my explorations and adventures working with healing energy on both myself and others. I have changed the names of some clients in the interests of confidentiality.

Welcome to my world!

Chapter 1

What I Know versus What I Believe

The only thing I know for sure is what I have experienced—or at least my perception of what I have experienced. This includes knowledge gathered with my sense perceptions, mental perceptions, and spiritual perceptions. These are my own discoveries gathered from living in the world. There are times when I feel that my life is a metaphysical science experiment. So much of what I didn't think was real has since become part of my journey through life. Let me start at the beginning to give some idea of my background.

I was raised with a metaphysical orientation. My father was well versed in esoteric studies and provided a family environment that encouraged free inquiry into the mystical part of life. I remember encountering a book by Joseph Murphy* in my father's den when I was fourteen, and I was fascinated by it. I loved to read about the powers of the mind and about miraculous happenings, but even though I found them entertaining, I didn't actually believe anyone practiced these ideas. But it was highly stimulating and interesting to think about them.

I'll never forget something my father said to me when I was a little girl: "In life, don't be so closed-minded that you are not open

1

to new ideas. But don't be so open-minded that your brains fall out." I'm happy to say that my brains are still intact. At least, that's my opinion. I still maintain a good bit of skepticism, but I have seen and experienced so much more than I ever believed was possible since my father uttered those meaningful words to me.

As a teenager, I was caught between fascination and denial, because at that time, if I came face-to-face with individuals who claimed to be adept at those weird and wonderful things I was reading, I would immediately judge them to be quacks, charlatans, and frauds. I just knew they were out to take money from people who were foolish enough to believe in them. Suckers! Awfully judgmental for a child—or anyone, for that matter—I guess I feared losing my brains, as my father had warned. If I had met a person like the one I am now back then, I can't even imagine what I would have thought.

My adolescent angst softened up and eased as I grew older, allowing me to relax my resistance and expand my beliefs. I moved from judgment to an increasing sense of awe of those who practiced mysterious and mystical healing work based on manipulating subtle energies in the body. My hunger to understand and be able to replicate those feats was an unending yearning. I would see someone do something that absolutely amazed me, and all I desired was to have that ability.

In my relentless quest to understand energetic healing, I experienced barriers to belief. The cycle would proceed thus: I would take classes to learn these things, but I found that once I mastered them, I would think, *Big deal—if I can do it, then it must not be as wonderful as I imagined.* These self-doubts plagued every endeavor, leaving my accomplishments flat and unconvincing even to me. I realized later—after building this toolbox, as it were—these abilities were insignificant. I just kept plugging along, looking for the next big mystery to tackle. It was always eluding me somewhere in the distant future, and I continued to discount the importance of everything I was learning.

By the time I got to the place where I could fully appreciate these abilities, it dawned on me that my doubting attitude was driving my search for more and better. After decades of accumulating new techniques, ideas, and concepts, I eventually synthesized my own method. My method is based on several processes that I have learned from others, along with intuitions gleaned through my own self-practice and in practicing with clients. Sometimes I would be at a total loss, and I would suddenly become inspired by a thought out of left field. I have come to realize that out of left field is where the magic happens. God, the unconscious mind, angels, guides, or whatever form of spirit you care to name must live out in left field.

Throughout early adulthood, through fits and starts, I began to form the basic belief system I now hold. One of these foundational beliefs that has become a guiding principle for my life can be stated as follows: "I believe it is done to us *as we believe.*" That means that we are the creators of our own experience. This is more than just a passing proposition. I have actually *experienced* this to be true. So it has become something I know firsthand, more on the order of a realization through lived experience. I can comfortably compare this with other types of knowledge I have gained from others' experiences received secondhand.

Science tells us everything is energy. I believe that. I have been told that nothing is truly solid, that matter is composed of atoms, which are composed of subatomic particles, and that I breathe oxygen. Did I discover any of this on my own? Can I prove it on my own using my own senses? No. But I believe the claims of scientists who have studied these things, just as I have come to believe mystical healers who have pursued more esoteric knowledge. Understanding the limits of my own knowledge has been helpful in developing my belief system and opening myself to new possibilities. But I also have observed that this openness does not happen for everybody.

I realize how difficult it can be for some people to grasp energetic healing. They want a solid mechanism of action, thinking that knowing this somehow makes their experience real. This reality was brought home to me when I was treating an engineer for a variety of symptoms he was having. We were making progress. He was feeling better. Yet during his third session, he began to question me on the whys and hows of the improvements and the energy work. I told him that I really did not know how it worked. I quickly learned that you don't tell an engineer that you don't know how something works. When I said those words, his face fell, and that was the last I saw of him.

It was not my intention to discount his questions. For me, the mechanisms of action were not important since we were getting results. Besides, you can't see the energy; you can only see the effects—so why did it matter? *After all, I reasoned, I don't understand how my car runs or how my computer, TV, and cell phone work. But I know they do, and I use them without worrying about the intricacies of the technology behind them.*

I experienced a major shift and breakthrough in my beliefs once I learned about the the Science of Mind* philosophy. I studied for four years and became a licensed practitioner in the Church of Religious Science during the late 1980s. This experience provided me with the basic scaffold upon which I built my overall belief system. I believe I have manifested much in my life through thought, including freedom from debt even without employment.

On one occasion, I was in a great deal of debt and had no idea how I would be able to repay the loan. I had entered a business partnership with someone I shouldn't have trusted and ended up owing over $100,000. *Oops!* I used principles I learned while studying *The Science of Mind* textbook. I knew the low paying job I had at the time wouldn't allow me to pay off the debt. I needed more wisdom than I had to deal with this situation. Once I felt secure that the problem would be handled without my interference of doubt and limiting beliefs, I gave the problem to God. I made a deal with God to figure it out and send me the money. My commitment was to put every penny I didn't need to survive toward the debt. Almost immediately, some investments that I had began to soar in value. Stocks split two and three times. I received special dividend checks in the mail. People repaid money I had forgotten I'd loaned out. Faith and belief are the power behind creating anything.

There are also things that I haven't manifested, and it isn't through lack of effort. I have asked myself and others throughout the years, "Why?" I believe the failure to manifest certain desires is due to deep-seated, underlying energy that contradicts what I have attempted to create. These are not conscious beliefs. If they were, I would have succeeded. My current belief (my beliefs change as I learn more) is that past-life issues *might* affect this lifetime. Ancestral issues or genetic programming *might* affect our lives, and unconscious beliefs *might* limit our conscious decisions.

I also believe that certain personal details, such as our names and birth dates, play a part in the creation of our lives. My father was a teacher of a study called the Science of Characteristics. It was based on the meaning of numbers and letters. Many people ask me the meaning of my name. My father used this study to create the name that would give me the best chance to actualize the potential of my birth date. In this study, letters contain the potential for certain abilities. Numbers contain capacities. When the capacity of the number is matched with the abilities of the letters, one supposedly is more easily able to actualize one's potential.

I grew up learning this school of thought, but I rejected it upon studying the Science of Mind, which I found to be much less limiting in its view. I was taught that we have the potential to have, be, and do anything we desire, as we are co-creators with All That Is, or what you might call God.

I believe we have the ability to create anything we desire as long as we are free of limiting beliefs. Here is the rub: How can you know if there are limiting beliefs if they are not in your conscious mind? That is what I do. I find the limiting beliefs and help my clients to release them. How do I do that? I access the information from the body using applied kinesiology.* The mind has opinions, but the mind is often wrong. Using logic is often a hindrance. By asking questions—usually silently, using telepathy—I use a form of muscle testing, applying pressure to the client's outstretched arm. Only yes and no answers are revealed. When the arm locks and I am unable to push against the resistance, I interpret that as a no. If the client is unable to resist the pressure, then that signifies a yes answer. (For those of you who are familiar with this process, this might sound backward. Most practitioners use a strong arm for a yes and weak for no, but this was not how I was originally trained.)

I also believe that astrology affects us. Astrology is much more than knowing your sun sign. I probably know just enough to be dangerous. I've studied a bit here and there, and I've been astounded at times at what I've learned. There are many excellent astrologers out there. As in any field, some are better than others. I've had people look at my natal chart (where all the planets were at the moment of my birth as viewed from the place I was born), and some have misinterpreted aspects because they didn't take the entire chart into consideration.

I have three planets in my twelfth house, including the sun. In some books, it says the twelfth house is the House of Sorrows. According to *The Encyclopedia of Psychological Astrology* by C. E. O. Carter, "The 12th house is traditionally styled the house of sorrow, and afflictions in it will not only cause grief and misfortune, but also tend to bring the native in contact with the sad aspects of life." I've read other sources that suggest those of us with planets in the twelfth house might be prone to chronic sadness and disillusionment. Does this indicate that my life is doomed to continual unhappiness? I sure hope not! There are also writings that suggest the twelfth house represents the unconscious and mystical side of us.

From all I've read and lived, I now believe that those of us with planets located in the twelfth house are more closely connected with past-life issues that affect us in this lifetime. There was a time when I didn't believe in past lives at all. When my life became affected quite dramatically due to past-life memories, I assumed everyone had these issues. My current belief is that many of us with planets in our twelfth house are more dramatically affected than others. So far, this has been my experience, but I am open to changing that belief when proven otherwise.

I recently read a book about Edgar Cayce, where the author mentioned a connection between astrology and past lives. For those of you unfamiliar with Edgar Cayce, he lived from 1877 to 1945. He learned how to put himself into a trance-sleep and would answer questions from this state, often diagnosing illness and prescribing cures. He had no memory of what was said once he awoke. In the book, *There is A River* by Thomas Sugrue, a gentleman named Mr. Lammers questioned Edgar regarding astrology and horoscopes. In his waking state, Edgar believed it was all fake. After the trance induced session, Mr. Lammers revealed what had come through. "You say this is my third appearance in this "sphere," and that I still have some inclinations from my last life . . . the solar system is a cycle of experiences for the soul. It has eight dimensions, corresponding to the planets . . . the subconscious is the record of the soul . . . our astrological influences from the planets . . . will be . . . according to the experiences we have had there . . ."

As I read this section of the book, I wondered if the transits that occur in our horoscopes are highlighting certain aspects within our natal chart, that allow past-life issues to come into our current experience. While this is still unclear to me, I find it an interesting subject to contemplate.

I was once working on a young woman, when I intuitively felt that her emotional issues were due to past lives. I asked her what her belief was in that area. She said she had been thinking that might be the case but couldn't talk to anyone about it, because her friends and family didn't feel comfortable discussing the idea of past lives. I then asked her if she knew anything about her natal chart. Though she didn't know much about astrology, she'd had a chart done many years ago. The astrologer hadn't spoken English, so the information had come to her through an interpreter and hadn't been particularly clear. I explained my beliefs regarding the twelfth house, and this seemed to stimulate her memory. She recalled being told that because of something regarding the twelfth house in her chart, she would suffer from sadness and depression. That was her fate.

It saddens me to hear anyone being given such a negative forecast. I shared my thoughts that her problems might have more to do with past-life issues. These usually can't be cleared if we are working with the conscious mind. As we continued the session, I found three past-life issues that appeared to be affecting her. Usually when people tell me they have had a particular belief or problem throughout their entire life, with no logical reason for feeling that way, it often ties back to either a past lifetime or ancestral/genetic issues. More about that later.

I believe all conditions can be relieved. That doesn't mean I have the ability to do so 100 percent of the time. Unfortunately, I'm still human. (Perhaps I should say "fortunately," or I wouldn't still be here.) But I always tell people that if I can't help them, then there is someone else who can. Never give up. You just need to find the right facilitator.

I say this because I was once told, "There is no hope," following an injury. That is the last thing anyone ever wants to hear. In my case, it wasn't a death sentence. I was expected to give up hope for a life of normal activity. If anyone has ever said to you, "There is no hope," he or she might be wrong. It's been said that if a doctor tells you that you have a limited time to live because of a particular diagnosis—whether it's three months, six months, a year, etc.—then find another doctor, because that one obviously doesn't know how to help you!

Many people say positive thinking is the key. I disagree. I don't believe that it is healthy to keep up a cheery front in an effort to be positive when that is not the truth. In fact, I think that is one of the causes of serious illness.

When you are focusing on the negative but have the ability to choose thinking in a more positive manner, then by all means, do so. It can make a world of difference in the energy you send out. As you send energy out, it manifests to attract and create circumstances of a similar vibration. But there are times when it seems no hope exists. It is unhealthy to lie to the world (and, more significantly, to yourself) and pretend that things are fine. It's extremely important to be honest. That doesn't necessarily mean going around to everyone you know and moaning and complaining about what is happening. It means recognizing there is a problem or issue that you are not happy about and doing something to correct the issue.

When we hold it in and suppress it, then it eats away at us from the inside out. It doesn't disappear. Denial can be dangerous. Acknowledging the hurts and processing them in whatever way we are able is the only healthy solution, in my opinion.

To go ten steps further, I don't believe that our issues die when we do. I believe they stay on this third-dimensional plane to be resolved. How are they resolved? It could be in another lifetime, it could move down the genetic line to another member of the family, or it could glom on to an unsuspecting individual who has a similar energy that attracts the issue. There might be a myriad of other possibilities that occur that I'm not aware of at present, or I could be totally wrong about the whole thing. That's what makes life interesting. There is often no definite answer. Why? Perhaps because it's done to us as we believe and we all have differing beliefs.

Chapter 2

My Journey into Quackdom

My journey began in earnest at the age of twenty-two. I was in my last year at UC Santa Cruz. It was a Sunday morning in November. I worked in the dining-hall kitchen and was the first one there. I enjoyed my job and took pride in it. When I arrived, I noticed a stack of crates filled with produce in the center of the room, so I walked over to the crates to put them in the walk-in refrigerator. A note with my name on it lay on top, telling me not to worry about moving them, because they were too heavy.

I thought, *I'm healthy. I'm strong. I lift weights. I can certainly put them away.* I began to carry the crates across the kitchen into the refrigerator. I always wanted to give 110 percent. That's the way I was raised. Do more than they expect, and it will pay off in the end. I intended to surprise my supervisors. There were five crates, and the first four were no problem. As I carried the last one in, I put it down for a second to catch my breath, because they really were heavy. I lifted the crate up above my head to stack it on top of the other four, and *bam!* I felt as if I had been shot in the back. I heard something pop, and I remember seeing stars as I fell to the floor.

I was probably unconscious for just a few seconds. When I opened my eyes, my first thought was *What happened?* I tried to move, but the pain was incredible. I had never hurt so much in my life. I realized you really do see stars with the pain. I had thought that only happened in cartoons.

I tried to stand up, but I couldn't. Suddenly, I remembered the note that had told me not to lift the crates. I felt an overwhelming sense of guilt. I was afraid I would get in trouble. Looking back now, I can see that thought made no sense at all, but that was the fear that gripped me. It took a few minutes, but I was able to get myself to an upright position sort of. I scrawled a note saying I wasn't feeling well and wouldn't be able to work that day. I somehow made my way back to my dorm room.

Fortunately, it was almost the end of the school term. Believing I had strained a muscle and would soon be good as new, I stuck it out the best I could. At the end of the term, I went home for the winter break, but I was not able to return to school. The pain wasn't getting better. I had tremendous pain not only in my back but also shooting down both legs. I went to see my doctor, and thus began my journey into hopelessness. Though it was a long time ago, there are moments that are burned into my memory.

One of those moments was the response of the doctor who told me what I had experienced was impossible. I mentioned the pop I'd heard from my back while lifting the crate. He said it was not possible, because I was too young for anything to pop. I told him I had pain shooting down both legs, and he told me it had to be one leg or the other. There was no way both legs could be affected, he insisted. He gave me a prescription for muscle relaxants and an anti-inflammatory medication to help with the pain and told me to rest until it felt better. I was scheduled to see him again in two weeks.

For the next two weeks, I lay on the floor, taking the pills but receiving no relief whatsoever. The only difference was now my mind was fuzzy. I couldn't think clearly.

I went back to the doctor at the appointed time, and I told him the pills were not working. He asked me what type of exercise I had been doing. I reminded him that he had told me to rest and had said it would get better. I informed him that the only thing I had been doing was lying on the floor. Any movement was excruciating. I had barely made it into his office, and I needed help getting there.

He called me lazy and said I needed to stop babying it. I insisted that if I could, I would move more, but it just wasn't possible with the intensity of pain I was experiencing. That was when he told me if that were the case, then I would just have to get used to living in excruciating pain for the rest of my life, because it would never get better. Then he ran off a verbal list of what I would never be able to experience.

Back in those days, I trusted doctors, and I thought he was serious. He told me to come back in a couple of weeks to see how things were progressing. By the time I arrived home, I had I replayed his words in my head several times. I thought my life was over. I went into a deep depression. If at the age of twenty-two all I had to look forward to was pain, then I didn't want to live.

Two weeks later, when I showed up in his office as a deeply depressed mass of pain, he looked at me and said, "Why do you look so sad?"

Seriously? The visit before, he had sent me home with no hope for any kind of future, telling me all the things I would never be able to do, and he didn't think it would affect me? He wrote out a prescription for antidepressants, handed it to me, and sent me off. He barely spoke to me other than telling me there was nothing he could do.

I walked out into the hall and tore up the prescription. Maybe he couldn't help me, but someone could, and I would find that person. The thought that occurred to me many years later was that he assumed I was malingering. He didn't even take X-rays to see if there was any damage. Perhaps he was using some psychological technique he had learned to try to motivate me to get moving. He had said I was too young for this to happen, after all. Unfortunately for me, he was wrong.

More than a decade later, as I was studying Oriental medicine, I learned that when a patient complains of back pain with sciatica and says the pain is running down both legs (as mine was), he or she might be malingering. The pain will usually travel down one leg or the other. Ah ha! So this was why he'd thought I was lying. What he didn't know at the time was that I had two herniated disks—one on the right side and another on the left. But no one bothered to check, because I was allegedly too young for this to happen.

Eventually, I went to chiropractors for treatments. At least they gave me hope. Five years after the initial injury, I was given an MRI and told I had ruptured two disks. Finally someone believed me! From this situation, I learned how important it is to validate the experiences of those who put their trust in me as a practitioner.

Chapter 3

Mr. Miyagi and Me

Did you ever see the original *Karate Kid* movie? There is a scene near the end of the movie where Daniel gets hurt during the karate tournament and asks Mr. Miyagi to help him. Mr. Miyagi puts him on a table, rubs his hands together, and places his hands on Daniel's leg. Daniel looks at Mr. Miyagi in surprise and says something about Miyagi's hands feeling hot on his leg. After a short time, Daniel, though not perfect, limps back into the ring, well enough to continue the tournament. At that moment, I decided if this technique Mr. Miyagi was doing was real, then I wanted to learn what it was and how to do it.

Not long after that, I was attending a Whole Life Expo in Pasadena. As I walked through one of the aisles, a woman asked me if I had ever heard of Reiki.* This was in 1985, and back then, I hadn't heard of it. She offered to give me a brief demonstration of it, so I sat in a chair in front of her, and she placed her hands on the tops of my shoulders. Immediately, I felt tremendous heat radiating from her hands. I knew this was what I had been looking for. Then and there, I signed up to learn this mysterious healing method.

Two weeks after that, I walked into the room where I would get my Reiki attunement* and be able to help myself and others heal.

Odd things happened that weekend. As I walked into the building to meet the teacher (called a Reiki master), her son looked at me and said, "Oh, you are a healer."

I turned around to see whom he was addressing, but there was no one behind me.

He said, "No, you. I can see you are a healer."

I shook my head. *What a bunch of nonsense*, I thought. *He probably says that to everyone who walks in, to make them feel important.*

I don't like that kind of manipulation, and I didn't care for the remark. But when I shook my head, he had looked puzzled and said, "Well, you do massage or something with healing, right?" I shook my head again, still thinking he was being insincere, but he insisted, "No, you heal people. I can see it."

In that moment, I felt a shift. I could feel his confusion as I continued to deny what he was saying. I knew he was telling the truth, but I didn't understand why. Though I was not a healer and had no idea what he was talking about, today I can honestly say that I think he was picking up on something that I was oblivious to back then.

Throughout the two-day workshop, I experienced a couple of notable sensations. During the attunement process (a ritual that opens the channels for the healing energy to flow), I felt a real, honest-to-goodness, palpable feeling moving down my spine. As it was occurring, I asked myself if there was any way I could be imagining it. But no, it was too strong a sensation to not be real. But I was still skeptical.

In class, I listened as people talked about the heightened energy in the room and about their angels and spirit guides and other energetic modalities they were practicing and working with, and I found myself thinking, *I'm in a room with a bunch of looney tunes. All of these wackos and crazies actually believe that all this stuff is real. Yikes! How did I get mixed up with these freaks?*

At some point, the Reiki master asked the group, "Do you all feel the energy? Can you feel it changing as more of you are being attuned?" Everyone around me was smiling and nodding.

Oh great, I thought. *They are not only crazy but also a bunch of liars. I don't feel a thing. There's no change in the energy. They can't feel anything either, but they don't want her to know that, so they just agree with her.* I have negative reactions when I feel people are lying, so all this talk definitely put me in a less than joyful state of mind.

I thought back to the original experience that had caused me to sign up for this class, and I made the decision to get whatever I could from the workshop. I did my best throughout the rest of the weekend to be as open-minded as possible. Choosing to put aside my negativity for the time being, I decided I would put this stuff to the test later. The other students, besides being crazy people, seemed friendly, so I elected to enjoy myself from that point on.

Then, in the last few minutes of class, something happened. Suddenly, I was enveloped by the most amazing sensation of love.

It was peace and joy and bliss.

It was everywhere.

It ran in and through me, and I wanted to bask in it for the rest of my life.

It was real.

No question about it—everything they said was real.

The energy.

The love.

It was all there, and now I could feel it. Finally!

What followed was one of the saddest things I'd ever heard. The Reiki master said, "The class is over. I wish you all the best." Everyone got up to leave.

I sat there thinking, *But I just got it! I finally feel it. I want more!* But that was it. I still didn't know if anything had changed other than feeling the bliss in that moment. Supposedly I would be able to help people just by using my hands. For the next few days, I tested and retested myself. I had been told during the class that whenever I touched anything living, the Reiki energy would just turn on. The living things (people, plants, and animals) I touched would draw through me whatever energy they needed. It wasn't *my* energy but

Universal Life Force. I did notice that when I touched anyone, my hands would get warm, if not hot. Since my hands were usually cold, this was a notable change.

Soon after attending the class, I was asked to volunteer at a health fair, giving free demonstrations, because another class was soon to be offered. I was happy to participate. It would give me a chance to see if strangers felt anything from my hands.

My first "victim" that day gave me an unforgettable experience. An elderly gentleman approached the booth where I was standing, so I asked him if he wanted to experience Reiki. He declined. I assured him there were no strings attached, and all he had to do was sit there and see if he felt anything. Again, he declined. I really wanted to get my hands on somebody, so I continued. "If nothing else, it'll give you a few minutes to sit down and rest your feet." He finally relented.

He sat down, and I asked him if he was experiencing any pain. He told me his neck was stiff, and he was unable to turn it to the left. I was excited! I could now test this magical power. I gently put my hands on his neck, and I concentrated hard to take his pain away. Concentration is not part of the Reiki protocol, but I really wanted to take his pain away. I could feel my hands getting warm. After about ten minutes, I took my hands off his neck, and I asked him, "How do you feel?"

"I told you nothing was going to—" But as he began to speak, he moved his neck back and forth freely. "Hmmm," he continued, "now I can move my neck. Hey, that's pretty good. Thanks." And he went on his merry way. Unfortunately, I couldn't move my own neck for the next week.

That was my own fault, and I spent about six months or so taking on everyone's pain, which was my intention, as I worked on various people. Well, it wasn't really the intention for *me* to take it on, but I didn't know a few things back then that I should have learned. I had been taught that the energy only went in one direction—through me to the other person—so the practitioner didn't ever have to worry about getting sick or hurt. As it turned out, that was not quite true. Or at least it wasn't true in my case.

I finally overcame this problem when I learned that I needed to consciously realize it wasn't *my pain* to take away. That knowledge made a huge difference in my experience. Years later (decades later, actually), I learned how to clear other people's energy from me and disconnect from them by cord cutting* and other methods. (I discuss this in length in another chapter.) Oh, sigh—live and learn, sometimes the hard way.

Chapter 4

Unexpected Left Turn

The decision to study alternative medicine happened quite unexpectedly. A decade after dropping out of college because of the back injury, I was at least well enough to consider completing my education. I decided to go to school locally, so I signed up at California State University in Los Angeles to finish my degree in theater arts. My final quarter included a new class never before offered. It was taught by Dr. Moon, an acupuncturist. The class was open to all acting and dance students, with the intention of teaching us how to heal ourselves. The emphasis was on healing injuries that occurred during or prior to a performance.

One of the first things Dr. Moon demonstrated was based on Touch for Health principles. According to this modality, each organ in the body has a correlation to a specific muscle group and certain acupuncture points. He tested the strength of a muscle to test the energy of an organ. One of the dancers volunteered to be a guinea pig as he explained and demonstrated the theory. He asked her to hold her arm straight out in front of her, and he pushed down on her wrist, but at one point, she was unable to resist the force. He asked, "Why is your deltoid so weak? You are young. You should be strong." He tested her other arm, which was easily able to resist as he tried to push it down.

I heard him say to himself, "Oh, her intestine is out of balance." He once again pushed down on the weak arm, which she couldn't hold up. He gently brushed a few upward strokes on her torso, to the side of her navel. He had her hold her arm up, and this time, she was as strong as ever and able to easily resist while he pushed it down. I watched as her eyes grew wide in amazement.

"Do that again!" she exclaimed. So he brushed the same spot on her body, but this time, he lightly brushed in downward strokes. She held her arm straight while he easily pushed it down. He repeated the exercise of brushing up on her body, and he tried to push her arm down, but it remained strong and able to resist.

Though she stood staring at him with her mouth gaping open, I was at least ten times more impressed with what I had just seen. In that moment, I knew I had to learn this new technique.

I asked him what this was called. He said, "It's based on acupuncture meridians." Though I would be graduating at the end of the quarter, I couldn't wait that long. I went home that night and began research to find out where I could learn acupuncture. Joyfully, I found out that classes were starting soon at Samra University of Oriental Medicine.

It would take four more years of school to earn the master's degree offered. I didn't care. I needed to know how to do this muscle-testing stuff, and I wanted to learn as soon as possible. The classes overlapped. While finishing up my bachelor's degree, I began the new school. I had no idea what I was getting into. Not only were we learning acupuncture and all the anatomy, physiology, chemistry, physics, pharmacology, etc., that was necessary, but we also had hundreds of herbs and formulas to learn as well—and in Chinese! I had no clue how intense it would be. I just wanted to learn how to muscle test.

Imagine my surprise when, two years into the program, I asked one of my professors, "When do we learn how to muscle test?"

"Do what now?" he asked, confused by my question.

I shared my story with him of what had brought me into the program. He laughed as he enlightened me by saying, "We don't teach that here. You can learn that in a weekend."

What! I thought. I had two more years of school to learn something I wasn't interested in, and I wouldn't even get what I wanted. How had this happened? I was devastated, but only for a moment. Okay, maybe it was more like a couple of hours, but then I got to thinking that it was no accident I had ended up there. My voices confirmed it. I heard something within me say, *You are here for a reason.*

I must admit that even though I don't like sticking needles in people, I learned a tremendous amount of theory that I appreciate and use constantly. Once I finally graduated and took my state board exams to become licensed as an acupuncturist, I could begin my real training. I signed up for a one-week intensive to learn Touch for Health with the founder of the modality, Dr. John Thie. I would show up early in the mornings, and he and I would have a short chat before class began. He gave me sound advice during one of our conversations. He said, "Whenever you have the opportunity, study with the original creator of a technique or modality. Each person who teaches it will color it with their own beliefs whether they intend to do so or not. It's always best to get it in the purest form possible." I have attempted to follow this wisdom whenever I have had the opportunity to do so.

Chapter 5

Lessons Learned

While writing this book, I had an eye-opening experience. I sent a client an account of our work, asking for permission to use it here. The response I received shocked me. I was not given permission to use the story, and I won't, but I will share this. The individual noted several criticisms regarding my version, including the belief that the way I had written it made him sound unstable. While the person admitted the session had been helpful, he believed my description of it took away all the good feelings from that time. I reread my account several times and couldn't find anything that I'd written indicating he was unstable or supporting any of the other claims he had cited.

The response really threw me for a loop. I had a hard time getting over the impact of the response. Needing some understanding, I called a friend who happened to be a doctor of psychology and read him my version. I said nothing about the circumstances but asked his opinion of what I had written. He thought it would be a good addition for this book. I revealed that I was unable to use the story, because the person involved thought I suggested instability in my account. My psychologist friend assured me the client's response had nothing to do with what I had written. There was no instability indicated in the individual. (The thought that he was unstable had never even crossed my mind.) Some of what the client had complained of was in complete opposition to what I had written.

He told me that he quite often saw this in his own practice. There are some people, when healed, who cannot face their own past thoughts, words, and beliefs. The seriousness is too much for them to handle. This causes them to unconsciously deny their own past experience.

In Oriental medical school, I learned that it was important to thoroughly document patients' symptoms, because they tend to forget they ever suffered from certain conditions once they are gone. For example, when a patient came in with a laundry list of symptoms, it was protocol to write each one down, including as much detail as possible. The reason was twofold: mainly so that we could understand and treat the underlying condition but also to ask the patient on subsequent visits how he or she was progressing. I was surprised how often patients developed amnesia regarding prior symptoms. When I asked people if anything had changed since the previous visit, most replied, "Not really." When I listed their previous complaints, they quite often had forgotten they had suffered from those issues. Here is an example of such a session.

"Mrs. Smith, has anything changed since your last treatment?"

"I don't think so. Everything is pretty much the same."

"How are the reoccurring headaches?"

"Oh, I don't have them anymore."

"And the upset stomach after meals?"

"No, my digestion is fine now. Hmm. That's right—I used to have a problem with that, didn't I?"

"Do you still suffer leg cramps at night?"

"No. In fact, I haven't woken up once since my last visit, and I no longer have insomnia either. Funny, I hadn't thought of that."

I was used to experiencing scenarios similar to this regularly. I think it's part of the human condition to forget how bad things were once they are better. Unless one likes to complain a lot and hold on to his or her story, people tend to forget. I consider this a good thing.

Another common occurrence is not recognizing that issues and behaviors have changed, even though the changes are apparent to those around us. Here is an example of what I mean.

When I was earning my Reiki master title, my teacher required that I document one hundred cases. I was to give one hundred people three free sessions each and write up a report on each case. (As I later came to learn, this was an unusual request. Most teachers do not require this much work. If you are interested in practicing Reiki, please do not let this information deter you.) In any case, I learned quite a bit from the experience. Most of all, I learned that each session is different from the last—not just from one person to the next but also from one session to the next with the same individual. It is typical for the first session to work on physical or surface-layer issues, the second session is deeper emotional or mental issues, and the third session reaches deeper soul-level issues. This is not true in every case but occurs often enough to make a note of it.

I worked on a couple who did not recognize their own changes but saw dramatic improvement in their partner. The husband wanted to feel more relaxed. His energy felt tight and wound up as I worked on him. He had two jobs and was going to school at night. His energy was go, go, go. His wife had her own business and worked from home but lacked motivation. Instead of working on her business, she sat around playing video games all day.

After giving them each three Reiki treatments, I asked them individually if they noticed any change. He said not much had changed for him. He did find himself to be more relaxed but noted his wife was like a different person. When he came home at night, instead of playing video games, she would be on the computer, working. There was a dramatic improvement in her behavior, and their relationship felt more harmonious, in his opinion. When I questioned her, she told me she had not had the remarkable change that she saw in her husband, even though she felt more motivated to work and wasn't interested in playing video games. He, however, was a completely different person, she said. He had even mentioned to her that now he knew how their cat felt, just being able to relax without a care in the world.

When I was learning acupuncture, one of my professors shared a story of one of her patients. The patient was a young woman with a terrible temper. She didn't get along with members of the family, and they all avoided her as much as possible. After a few treatments, the professor questioned her patient regarding improvement, but the woman denied feeling any shift. The funny thing was, my professor received calls from several of the family members, asking what she had done to change the young woman and make her so kind. For the first time, her family enjoyed being around her.

As you can see from these stories, energy work can affect more than just the physical body. It can help to balance the mind and the emotions. It's not typical in our culture to focus on becoming self-aware. In fact, we live with many distractions in our lives, such as sports, TV, movies, social media, computer games, etc., that keep us from recognizing and assessing what is going on within our own being. When changes occur, we aren't even cognizant of the fact.

The world is said to be a reflection of what is going on inside of us. While we know it's not helpful to try to change the mirror, in order to change ourselves, sometimes it's helpful to check the reflection to see if *we* have changed. I often ask my friends to give me their thoughts about me in certain areas, because I know we all have blind spots when we self-assess. I have three suggestions for you if you decide to do that:

1) Be prepared to handle whatever they say.
2) Listen without being defensive.
   (and most importantly)
3) Be careful whom you ask.

Chapter 6

To Infinity and Beyond

I t was December 1986. I was in a class that met weekly for a couple of months. The theme was psychic development. We practiced different exercises to become more intuitive. Prior to this course, I had read about astral projection, the ability to travel outside of the body. It sounded fantastic, and I deeply desired to have this experience. I asked the instructor if we could learn how to project ourselves outside the physical form and travel to distant lands in one of our classes. She agreed. I thought she had forgotten as the weeks progressed. She hadn't, and I was delighted when she announced at the beginning of class a few weeks later that we would practice astral projection.

As we prepared to take flight, I was seated on the floor, leaning against a chair. Our teacher began by having us relax our bodies and focus on our breathing. Then she began what sounded like a hypnotic induction. She gave us suggestions to travel to the place we would most like to be, and since I had no idea where that might be, I didn't focus on anywhere in particular.

At the end of the exercise, I found myself back in the room, but it seemed like a million years had passed from the time I had closed my eyes. I looked at everyone else, thinking they must have had the same extraordinary adventure. The students all shared their stories of where they had gone and what they had experienced. My father, who was also a student in the class, said he had flown over the Hawaiian Islands. He had been able to zoom down at will to any of the islands he desired and zoom back up into the sky. Some people had gone to their favorite vacation spots, while a couple of others had gone to their respective hometowns. Some had traveled to places they had never been but had always dreamed of one day going. I kept waiting to hear someone describe something similar to my experience, but it never happened. When everyone else finished telling their own story, I spoke up. As I write this in 2013, over twenty-six years later, I can remember this episode as though it happened yesterday.

As we began, I was breathing slowly, focusing on the sensation of air moving in and out of my nostrils. I heard our instructor counting from one to ten, when all of a sudden, I was surrounded by complete darkness. I was more conscious and aware than I had ever been. I looked all around (with what, I don't know, as I had no body and, therefore, no eyes, but look I did). I was seeking the light. *There's got to be a light somewhere*, I thought. *I keep hearing about a tunnel. It's got to be here somewhere.* As I continued to seek, I became hyperaware of the peace that surrounded me. It expanded to a feeling of overwhelming love.

I am one of the fortunate individuals on this planet who grew up with love. Though no thing or person is perfect in this life, including my family, I must say that I always felt loved as a child. Surrounded by darkness in that moment of incredible love, I thought about my childhood and the love I felt back then. I imagined the feeling I used to have as I walked in the front door of the house where I grew up with my family. I attempted to compare the love I had felt then with the love I was experiencing at that moment. There was no comparison—not even close. The love that enveloped me was like the ocean compared to the love I felt on this earthly plane, which felt like only a single drop.

In that moment, a knowingness infused my mind that *this* was home. It was where we all came from and where we would all end up again. The joy at that understanding was immeasurable.

I don't believe in a heaven in the clouds, with angels flying around, playing their harps. I never did. I also don't believe in a hell, ruled by a devil with a pitchfork living in a barbecue pit. I'm just stating my beliefs—or, rather, my nonbeliefs—with no intention of offending anyone else's beliefs.

I remember watching the character Fred Sanford on *Sanford and Son* grasping his chest as he feigned a heart attack, looking skyward and saying, "I'm coming home, Elizabeth." I had never understood what he meant by equating death with coming home. But now I understood. This was home: this magnificent, blissful space—or nonspace—of pure love.

I've heard and read many accounts about near-death experiences. Many are similar to each other in nature, including the idea of going through the tunnel, seeing the light, and being met by loved ones, guides, Jesus, the council of elders, or whoever is there as the reception committee. I've heard the stories of feeling the love and of those who were told it was not their time and they must go back, etc. Don't get me wrong—I believe each and every one is absolutely a real experience. I believe it is a valuable and significant experience, but now I have my doubts regarding the truth of where we go when we die.

I've read about soul families, how we make agreements to learn certain lessons, and how we have specific missions here on earth. I've read that for the most part, we choose our lives, our parents, and our challenges. I've learned that while we have free will, much is also predetermined. This is all possibly the truth. I can't deny it, because I have no proof. I also can't confirm it is the absolute truth.

The experience I had was not like anything I had ever read about. It was not similar to the accounts of others. First of all, there was no light. There was no other person; there was only the most pure sense of love one could ever imagine. It was a warmth as tangible as a warm blanket. It was soothing and comforting and ever present. As I became acclimated, I began thinking of questions. I asked why my mother had died so suddenly earlier that year. I asked about time. I had heard that time was an illusion and was not real. I couldn't understand how this could be, so I asked, and my question was answered.

Every time I asked a question—any question—I received an answer. The instant I formed the question in my mind, I saw, felt, and experienced the answer, completely. Here was the problem: when I came back into the awareness of my body, I was not allowed to bring back any of the information I had been shown. I could remember every question I had asked, and I could bring back every thought I had about each experience, but only those thoughts that I had generated in my own mind. If I had not initiated the thought, it was erased as I returned.

Here is what I do remember. I was shown the history of the planet. It was like a movie that was played backward, from the present moment to the beginning of the earth's formation. But unlike watching a movie, I somehow experienced every part of it—all of life. It was three dimensional, and I was part of all of it. When it finished, I remember thinking, *Wow! That was the history of the earth!* But then it started all over again, only this time, it was a completely different version. I thought, *The earth has had more than one life,* and as soon as I had that thought, I saw a third version of the planet's history. I can't tell you for sure if there was another one after that or not, but I was feeling so astonished and overwhelmed that I said, "That's enough. I just want to feel the love some more." And I did. Once again, I was surrounded and imbued with the sensation of the most exquisite bliss one could ever imagine. After basking in the love for what felt like millions of years, I was ready to ask more questions. Each moment that I was there seemed simultaneously like all time and no time. There is no way to communicate this sensation so that it makes sense, but while in that state, it felt natural and normal.

I have tried many times through meditation to get back to that state, but I have never been able to replicate the experience. I questioned it for many years, but I know what and how I felt, and it has altered my beliefs tremendously. I've heard and read about near-death and out-of-body experiences and have wondered why my experience differed so much from all the others. It made no sense until I read the book *The Disappearance of the Universe** by Gary Renard. I won't go into detail here, but I highly recommend the book. It helped give me an expanded perception of life.

One thing I know is that I was more aware than I have ever been, and I was in complete control of my experience. When I chose to be with the love, I was one with God, or love or whatever you want to call it. I felt as though I were there for eternity, and yet at any moment, I could choose something else. The instant I had a thought, that new thought would become my experience—totally and completely. Whenever I chose to change the experience, I would have another thought, and then that one would be my new experience.

So why or how did I come back? To tell you the truth, I wished I hadn't come back. But I came back with a definite knowingness that over there is the place where we all return, and that gave me peace.

As suddenly as it had begun, the experience ended. I was sitting on the floor with my back against a chair. I opened my eyes, and the instructor was in front of me, glancing at her watch. She paused but didn't see I had opened my eyes. She gently said, "Come back from wherever you are and become aware of your body. When you are ready, you may open your eyes."

I wondered why I had come back just before we were told to do so. It was an interesting coincidence. Maybe I wanted to beat the crowd. But in all honesty, I think it was because there was a higher part of me that was tuned into both worlds and wanted my lower self to know it was paying attention. While I'm in this body, in this dimension, I will never know. But maybe someday.

Chapter 7

I'm a Synthesizer

No, I'm not a musical instrument, but I suppose you knew that. What I mean is that I have synthesized a technique to release (primarily) emotional issues from the body. I have studied many energetic modalities and have since created my own technique based on several of them. I never set out to do this intentionally. It just evolved. After I graduated with my master's degree in Oriental medicine, I studied Touch for Health and Nambudripad's Allergy Elimination Technique* and other classes, based on using applied kinesiology* known as muscle testing. It took me two years of practice to become a competent tester. Many of the classes and workshops I studied gave a greater understanding of how the mind affects the body to both create and heal disease states. More importantly, these classes gave me good questions to ask the body in order to uncover the underlying issues.

As I learned techniques, I practiced them strictly as they had been taught. Eventually, I realized that certain aspects of some techniques could be combined with aspects of other techniques to give a more comprehensive treatment, depending on the case. My intention is to give the most all-inclusive treatment in the most concise manner and in the safest way possible. If my magic wand were all-powerful,

I would wave it with the intention of healing the client completely of all disease permanently and instantaneously. Unfortunately, that has yet to happen, but I'm optimistic that I am getting closer to that goal day by day.

Frustration hits me every time I hear someone talk about the healing process being akin to peeling the layers of an onion. I resist that thought, because on many occasions, I've seen instantaneous corrections in the body when there is a release of what I call the "energy of the disease program." I believe all illness has a specific energy frequency. When that frequency (or program) changes, then the body reflects the change on a cellular level. Similar to a computer virus, when the virus or program is corrected, the computer works correctly.

There are several reasons why it might take time to release the disease. One of the most limiting factors is the belief that it will take time. There are other factors, including the amount of energy the body has available to heal. The more life force one has, the easier it is to heal, especially with regard to a severe condition. Also of major importance is the ability to get down to the core cause. In my experience, there is an emotional issue at the core of most diseases. Finding and releasing this emotional factor can make all the difference. As I've said before, this is usually on an unconscious level of awareness, so trying to figure it out logically is illogical. That's why I've continued with my education so relentlessly. I'm constantly attempting to glean more information and ideas to add to my reservoir. I take the best of the newest techniques and put those in my invisible toolbox. Some things I learned directly from my clients during treatments.

One of the most dramatic sessions I had was with Dagne, who came to me with rheumatoid arthritis. At least, that was the diagnosis she had been given. As a woman in her thirties with four young children at home, it was important to her to have full use of her arms. Because of the pain in her right arm, she was unable to accomplish much of what she needed to do. Her rheumatologist, as a last resort, wanted to prescribe a strong steroidal medication. Because of the side effects, Dagne preferred not to take it, if at all possible. I tested her body for several things but could not come up with the cause of her problem. I am persistent when it comes to my work (you might call me stubborn), and I refused to give up.

I began to ask out-of-the-box questions. The first helpful piece of information that came up was that it was not her pain; it belonged to someone else. That was an eye-opener! Then we began a round of twenty questions to figure out whose pain it could be. It turned out to be the pain of her father, who had committed suicide many years ago. Though I had been taking classes in healing fifteen years prior to this session, I had never learned how to work on dead people. Here we go, from out of the box to out in left field.

I looked at her and asked if she knew how to proceed, because I didn't have a clue. She told me a little bit about her father and the emotional pain he had been in. I tested* and learned that he still needed healing from the pain and that forgiveness was required. Then Dagne had an idea. Her mother had just passed within the year, and she thought maybe her mother, being in the spirit world, could help her father. She tested yes when asked if this was the case. We called upon her mother and went from there. It appeared that her mother was able to help her father forgive himself and we spent some time sending him to the light and releasing his burdens. It became apparent that Dagne's pain had been his way of getting attention for the help he needed. Because we were winging it, I really can't tell you all that was said and done. I can tell you that at the end of that session, Dagne was free from the pain in her arm. Many years have passed since that session, and her pain has never returned. Pretty good quackery, if I do say so myself.

I later learned that working on ancestors is not unusual. I owe a huge debt of gratitude to Vianna Stibal, though I have never met her. She is the creator of a technique called ThetaHealing.* She has written books and teaches classes worldwide. My teacher of ThetaHealing, Marina Rose, is an amazing healer and teacher. She also teaches around the world, and it was an honor to study with her.

One of the most useful things I learned from ThetaHealing is finding the level of the cause. That means I ask where the issue originated. Usually, what we think of as the cause is not so. That is what I now believe after my years of practice. The mind is always trying to make logical sense, but I always listen to what the body says rather than the ego, or mind.

The four levels of cause are

1) this lifetime, including from conception to birth;
2) a past lifetime;
3) ancestral and genetic issues; and
4) soul level, which I find to be rare.

This Life

Vianna calls this Core Level. I ask if the issue began in this lifetime. If the answer is yes, then I find out if it occurred before or after birth. If before birth, then I ask in which trimester it began and continue to narrow it down further until we eventually get to what happened. Sometimes we don't need to know exactly what occurred, because the consciousness of the body knows, and the body has the ability to tune in to make the corrections when given the command to do so. I believe fetuses (and babies, for that matter) are fully conscious of everything that is occurring around them. The issues of many of my clients began while they were still in the womb or sometimes when they were only days old. Just because babies are unable to communicate what they are experiencing doesn't mean they are not completely aware of everything around them. Sometimes they are more aware than the rest of us.

Playing detective is often the most interesting and sometimes the most frustrating part of my job. I never know what I'm going to find. When I'm working with an issue from this lifetime after birth, I narrow down the year when it became an issue and ask the client what was going on in his or her life at that time. People will often say, "Nothing that I can recall," but as we continue, they will suddenly remember something important or traumatic that occurred that they hadn't thought of in years. Oftentimes, when that event is cleared out, there is a dramatic improvement.

Here's a story to illustrate. A friend of mine in his fifties had suffered from a severe case of motion sickness since childhood. He would get sick as a passenger in a car; therefore, he always had to drive. Standing on a dry dock and looking at the water made him queasy. Even watching a movie could cause the problem. Years ago, we went to see the movie *Twister* together in a theater, and we had to leave because he became so nauseous that he vomited in the men's room. A couple of years later, he tried to watch the movie on TV, and again he threw up. I finally persuaded him to let me work on his problem.

It took three separate sessions to completely heal his motion sickness. The first session, we determined through muscle testing, was to correct a physical problem of harmonizing his stomach with his inner ear. The second session involved his eyes and pituitary gland. The third session was different. Testing revealed the condition had begun when he was in the womb. I asked him if he knew of anything significant that had happened during that time. At first, he could think of nothing, but then he recalled that his grandfather and uncle had both drowned in a boating accident just before he was born. Upon asking his body if this was the cause of the motion sickness, I tested with a yes response. I worked on him to clear the traumatic memory from his body, and he hasn't had any motion sickness since that time, which was many years ago. He has even been on a few cruises, including one rocky ship that had to circumvent three hurricanes. He recounted to me how the ship swayed dramatically during parts of the cruise and how the dining room was often quite empty, as most of the passengers were seasick. But not him. He maintained a healthy appetite throughout with no problem whatsoever.

His mother and sister, however, have a great fear of being on any boat. When anyone asks them if they would consider a cruise, they scream, "*Titanic!*" I have no idea if their fear is related to the family trauma or not. They don't want me to work on them, because I'm a quack.

Past Lives

I'm not going to tell you that past lives do or don't exist. I always ask the question while working on a client, but even when the answer is yes, that doesn't mean it is so. Yes, there is a possibility that we are recycled, but even if that is true, I don't believe that lifetimes happen sequentially. What I have learned in various classes and through books, is that all lives are actually happening at once. There is only the now. Because we live in a time/space dimension, it only appears that time exists and is linear. I'm not interested in debating the issue. My focus is helping to facilitate a healing.

Another session taught me that sometimes working on future lives can correct a problem. I once tested a client whose issue was not apparently from this lifetime. We had already ruled out the other possibilities.

So I asked, "Past life?"

I received the answer no.

I rechecked. "This life?"

"No."

This discussion went back and forth a few times. I was at my wits' end, and out of frustration, I thought, *What's left?*

"Future life?" I asked just because I didn't know what else to ask, and the body gave me a yes.

Wow! This was a surprise. I had to retest that one several times to make sure I was getting a valid answer. I treated the issue of a future life, and the client's problem cleared up. Weird.

I have wondered if our past lives are really *our* past lives. One thing I truly believe is that when we die, if we still have issues, they remain on this plane. What happens to these unresolved issues?

My current belief is that they are waiting for resolution in some form. How do they get resolved? First, the issue has to be known. So someone must present with the problem. Who? My guess is that we are reborn with the issue or the problem continues down the genetic line in the form of DNA. In that case, when I ask for the level of cause, it shows up as an ancestral issue.

The first time I treated an ancestral problem was unintentional. I was working with a woman who had a serious case of eczema. She was middle aged, and since childhood, she had not worn shorts, skirts, dresses, or anything that revealed her legs. Also, she had not worn anything above the waist that didn't have long sleeves to hide her arms. I had never before seen a case of eczema so severe. To understand the texture of her skin, you would have to imagine pink alligator hide. Back in those days, I was still practicing acupuncture and herbology and just dabbling in energetic work.

After several visits with barely a change in her condition, I decided to try something different. I began to muscle test her, and I asked all kinds of questions. Something came up about the cause being related to something happening at the age of twelve. I asked her what had happened then. Though she couldn't think of anything significant at first, she then remembered that was the year her grandfather died. She had been close to him, and she shared several stories. Suddenly, she stopped talking and gasped. "My grandfather had eczema," she recalled. She had completely forgotten that fact. The severity of his condition now came back to her. I tested, and sure enough, her condition was associated with him. I had her touch spots on her skin that were affected, and we did some release work.

As the clearing work continued, I heard her stomach gurgling. I always love a physical response to confirm something is happening. At that moment, I didn't know if anything would change, but so far, nothing else had worked.

She returned to my office a week later. According to her, for the first time in almost forty years, her skin had begun to clear up. She was elated, as was I. I looked at the spots on her flesh, which were now slightly pink and smooth compared to what I had seen just days before. That summer, she was able to bare her arms and legs. Until that particular session, I hadn't realized the importance of asking about ancestors. It was many years later, after learning ThetaHealing, that I began questioning the body for ancestral causes on a regular basis.

When I test a person for genetic or ancestral issues, I sometimes ask, "How many generations ago did this begin?" I've gotten answers from one to well above one hundred. To clear the issue, the technique I find most reliable is ThetaHealing, but other techniques are helpful. I feel it's most effective to clear both the client with this problem and the ancestor with whom it began. I also attempt to clear the genetic line.

To explain briefly my technique, here is what I do. I go into a deep meditative state, I call in the ancestors, and then I mentally release all drama, trauma, hurt, and pain they caused to themselves and to others. I call upon All That Is (Creator, Source, God) to do this, and I mentally see waves of energy being released from the body. (Vianna Stibal, in her book *ThetaHealing*, mentions that one of the most important factors is witnessing the healing.) Then I release all of the drama, trauma, hurt, and pain others caused them and their loved ones. I do the same for the client until the healing feels complete. During that process, I often feel things shifting in my body, and sometimes the person I'm working on feels things releasing also. From those who are sensitive to energy, I hear comments such as "It felt as though something left my body." I might hear their stomachs gurgle, or they feel a wave of energy passing through them. I know it may sound bizarre to those of you who have not had this experience, but this is truly the feedback I receive. Of course, there are plenty of people who are relieved of their complaints yet feel nothing during the session. I find that individuals who meditate regularly often develop an increased sensitivity.

Perhaps the laws of karma cause us to be reborn and pay our debts, but I don't personally believe it to be as a punishment. Maybe it's so that our soul or being will experience the other side of what we might have previously dished out. One thing I do believe is that we are not resigned to suffering. If it is true that we come back to resolve the hurt we have caused, then once we understand it and forgive ourselves and all others, we can be released of the pain.

Forgiveness is huge. There are some people who never get better no matter how much I work on them or how hard I try. I asked in a meditation once why this is. The answer came back as follows: "You cannot override someone's lack of forgiveness." That makes sense to me because when I think of a few unsuccessful cases, I can recall the client saying, "I will *never* forgive (whoever)."

Here is my opinion regarding forgiveness*: It has nothing to do with the other person. Forgiveness is all about the one doing the forgiving. It is the willingness to let go of the pain. Release yourself from the anger, hurt, betrayal, or whatever the painful emotion is. It is causing *you* to suffer and not the other person. The other party will have to deal with his or her side of it his—or herself.

Maybe there is no such thing as past lives. Maybe what appears to be past lives are lives of people who have died whose unresolved energy lingers and attaches onto some unsuspecting soul. Even if this is the case, I doubt that it is a random phenomenon. Again, my personal belief is that *if* this is the case, the person getting glommed upon might have attracted that energy unconsciously. I do believe that our beliefs, both conscious and unconscious, affect our lives.

I studied Religious Science* in the '80s and early '90s and became a licensed practitioner. I still practice scientific prayer as it was taught in the book *The Science of Mind*.* It was then that I learned how powerful our thoughts are. Once I became aware of what I was thinking and what I was attracting and creating in my life, I took control over my life. I can't even imagine where I would be today had I stayed in the destructive path of negative thinking. So instead of blaming everyone for everything, I learned to turn within and change my stinking thinking.

I don't think it even matters if one believes in past lives or not in order for past-life healing to take place. Here is an example to demonstrate that point. A young man was dragged into my practice by his wife. She had been a client of mine who'd had a few successful treatments for various issues. When her husband was available, they came to see me for his motion sickness. He was extremely skeptical of my work, so I knew to be careful with what I said. I found miscommunication in his endocrine system that had occurred while he was in the womb. I did some work to correct the miscommunication, primarily using a technique called BodyTalk,* and his body tested that the work was complete. When I mentioned this, he asked in a skeptical tone, "You mean now I can let my wife drive and I won't get sick?"

I responded, "I honestly don't know. I hope that's the case. All I can tell you is that your body said it's corrected." I was more than a little apprehensive at this point because I knew he didn't trust me, and if nothing had changed, I was sure I would hear about it and so would his wife. So I double-checked. His body tested yes when asked if the treatment was complete. I asked his body if there was anything else we needed to do, and it said yes, but it was for another physical issue.

I asked him if he had another complaint that needed addressing. He didn't understand what I meant by that. I told him that although the motion sickness was corrected, there seemed to be another physical problem in his body that was bothering him. I told him it could be an injury or pain or something that was not functioning correctly. He then told me he had a hip problem. As I silently tested his hip, I got that this was a past-life issue. My inner voices cautioned me not to mention the idea of past lives. (I found out later that his fundamental Christian beliefs did not allow him to entertain the idea of reincarnation.)

When I asked him what he thought the cause might be, he told me he played basketball on the weekends. He thought he was probably overdoing it, and that was what caused the pain. When I silently asked his body if that was the cause or even a contributing source of pain, I got a response of no.

I let him know that his body indicated the problem was older than he was, and I wondered out loud what that might mean. He looked perplexed and said he didn't know. I was really hoping he would come out with the past-life idea himself. I waited for him to reconsider, but he was adamant. In an attempt to stall while he gave it more thought, I said, "Well, maybe it's in your DNA and is genetic. That would be older than you, right?"

"Right," he agreed, so I tested for an ancestral or genetic cause, but of course, that was not the case.

"What else could it be?" I asked, and I waited. He stared at me, and I think he caught on to what I was thinking, but he wouldn't say it. So I played dumb and said, "You know, I've heard people talk about past lives. Do you think that could be it?"

"No!" he quickly responded.

"Could we test for it anyway?" I hesitantly suggested.

"No!" he practically shouted.

I was stuck, not knowing what to do. Finally, I told him I had an idea, and I silently muscle tested, asking if we could clear this issue without his conscious knowledge that we were clearing a past-life problem. I got a clear yes answer, so I proceeded to clear it. When he left, he had no pain in his hip.

He called me a couple of months later to let me know not only that the hip pain had not returned but also that his motion sickness was completely gone. He was still playing basketball regularly without any pain, and he could enjoy being a passenger while his wife drove the car.

The skeptic in me is always so grateful when I hear the long-term results of these treatments. Because I don't know exactly *how* it happens, it continues to boggle my mind.

Chapter 8

My Reconnection

I saw Dr. Eric Pearl on TV a number of years ago being interviewed on a show called *The Other Side*. He talked about his healing abilities, and I was intrigued. I decided to make an appointment for a series of sessions.

During the healings, I closed my eyes as he held his hands over me. I saw a purple light, which is typical when I am in the presence of a healer. Other than that, I didn't feel much of anything. After one of the healing sessions, I complained of a pain in my neck, so he offered to give me a chiropractic adjustment. Within a few minutes, he adjusted almost every bone in my body. He had me lie down, sit up, stand, and turn this way and then that as me moved from one body part to the next. I mentioned to him that I had never had so many adjustments in so little time. As I drove home from that session, I felt as if I could fly. I had a wonderful feeling of energy and freedom throughout my body.

I bought his book *The Reconnection* and read it. It's a fascinating story, and I highly recommend it. I lent my copy to others a few times, and in each case, there were weird occurrences. I have since been warned that while a person reads the book, energies begin to work on the reader.

I had some computer trouble at the time I read the book, but I can't know for sure if the book was the cause. One of my friends said the light in her bedroom closet would suddenly turn itself on while she was reading the book. Someone else I lent the book to swore up and down that this strange event happened as she was midway through the book: She had just gotten into her car in the driver's seat, with a friend sitting in the passenger seat. As she held the car key in her hand, preparing to put it in the ignition, her car started on its own. Both she and her passenger freaked out.

After I met Dr. Pearl and had him work on me, I decided to have the Reconnection process done. It is a specific protocol that activates the body's axial system with the grid of the universe and the ley lines of the earth. Specifically, what does this mean? I don't know. But I will share my experience.

It was a hot day in July when my appointment time arrived. The woman doing the process worked out of her home. The room was not air-conditioned. I lay on a massage table in the heat of summer. I usually fare pretty well in the heat, so I didn't really mind the high temperature. As I lay on the table, the practitioner drew lines above my body. She explained to me that the lines used to be drawn directly on the body of the recipient, but there was a new protocol. For whatever reason, the experience was too strong for most people and was not appropriate. Now, she said, the lines were drawn over the body, and it was much easier to cope with the new energies.

The one thing that stands out in my mind clearly is how cold I became. My body felt like ice. There was absolutely no reason why I should have turned cold. There was no air-conditioning at all. Maybe a window was open or a fan was blowing, but the breeze in either case would have been warm. When she finished, I immediately felt the heat of summer again.

I later took a two-day class with Dr. Pearl, and there were times when I could feel his energy in the room. We had somewhere between one hundred and two hundred people taking the class together, with maybe thirty massage tables scattered about the room. During the two days, four or five people worked together, giving healing treatments using this new technique. When I was on the table with my eyes closed, I knew exactly where Dr. Pearl was. I didn't hear his footsteps, but I could definitely and clearly feel his energy. While lying on the table with my eyes closed, I felt him about twenty-five feet beyond my right shoulder. I don't know how I knew he was there, but I did. Just to be sure, I opened my eyes and sat up and turned around. There he was—exactly where I had felt him. I lay back down and closed my eyes.

Then I felt his energy moving across the room. It wasn't footsteps that alerted me—just an intense energy. It moved down the right side of my body toward my feet and beyond. He was approximately fifteen feet to my right. The energy stopped and moved toward my left. I could tell he still wasn't close to me. I followed the direction of the energy, and when the movement of the energy paused, I opened my eyes, sat up, and looked directly at him; he was now about twenty feet beyond me.

Once again, I closed my eyes while my practice group worked over me. Oddly enough, I didn't feel any of the energy from the group members. I only felt that of Dr. Pearl. The final time I opened my eyes was when I felt a strong increase of his energy. The vibration of energy running through me was intense but pleasant. I opened my eyes, and there he was, standing over my table. Mind you, he hadn't spoken a word, so it was not his voice that made me aware of his presence. There was something about his energy that I could feel.

Most facilitators of healing practices say the same thing: "If I can do this, anyone can." I used to believe these words. That notion was what kept me taking classes and workshops year after year, going from teacher to teacher to learn all these modalities as I saw them practiced. I made it a point to study with the best of the best. If I could learn directly from the originator of the modality, then I wanted to take the class from him or her.

In each case, though I learned quite a lot, I was never able to duplicate the results as well as I had hoped. It could be that my expectations were too high. But I think there was another explanation. I believe the modalities individuals teach came to them because those are *their* ways of doing it. Many of the classes were modifications or additions to other techniques previously studied by the instructors. I'm not saying that others can't learn and be as proficient in any of these techniques. I don't know that it will work as well for others or not, but it has not been my observation. Maybe each one of us who practices needs to make it our own to be our best. Or maybe that's my own experience because I needed to create my own style.

I'm not saying I didn't derive benefit from the class. I absolutely noticed a change in my body after the experience. Now when I'm scanning someone's energy field, I notice a distinct squeak in my arms. My interpretation of that squeak is that it's a buildup of congested energy in the client's field, creating an energetic block.

Another healer/teacher whose energy affected me dramatically was Alain Herriott. He taught a course called Quantum Touch—Core Transformation. This technique required placing one's attention in a specific spot in the center of your head, behind the eyes. When you are in that spot and follow the protocol, you can achieve miraculous results. I must admit, many amazing feats were accomplished during that weekend seminar.

Here is an example. At one point, we were to practice working on each other's shoulders. I worked on a woman who had limited range of mobility in her right shoulder. I asked her to show me how high she was able to lift her arm. She raised her arm so that it was at a ninety-degree angle to the floor. I used the method we were taught, and in my mind's eye, I could see her raising it to the point where it actually touched her ear. I knew without a shadow of a doubt she now had complete freedom of movement. I opened my eyes and, with complete confidence, told her to raise her arm again to verify the change. She lifted her arm with improved mobility, but not as far as I had believed it would go. She was delighted with the increased range of motion. Not me. I was angry.

Why did I fail? I wondered. I just *knew* she had full range of motion. Time was called to switch recipients. Now it was time for her to work on me. While my eyes were closed, I felt something changing in my shoulder. It seemed as though the muscles were moving under my skin. Something was comfortably stretching them out. I asked her what she was doing, and she explained that she was lengthening the bone.

Since I didn't have a problem with my arm and I'd had an experience that satisfied me, I asked if we could return to her problem. She agreed, so I asked her once again to show me her range of motion. She raised her arm straight up and rested it against her ear. Yes! This was what I had seen in my mind's eye. I hadn't failed after all. I had just been a little impatient. I suppose her body needed a bit more time to process the energy to make the change. Now I was satisfied.

The problem I had in the class was that my ability outside of the class was not nearly as successful. I noticed that in my hotel room, I wasn't able to locate or go into the specific spot in the brain as easily as I could with Alain in the room. The second morning before the class began, I complained to Alain that his energy was helping me do the process and that I wasn't able to do it on my own. I said, "Your energy is helping me get there."

"No, you are doing it. It's not my energy," he insisted.

"I can't do it without you," I stubbornly disagreed. "Your energy is putting me in that spot."

Then he surprised me by saying, "This is what it's like when I put you in there," and immediately, I was in a state of pure bliss. My head lightly buzzed. I could have lived in that state forever. All thoughts left my mind, and I experienced peace and joy.

"Okay? Got it?" he asked with a slight edge to his voice.

I attempted to respond with a resounding "Yes!" but I could only manage a hushed whisper, feeling the wonderful sensation that enveloped me. I dreaded the moment I would have to force myself to leave this incredible state of pure is-ness, but the class was about to begin, so I dragged myself back to what we call reality. I still believe that his energy field was affecting me throughout the class. But lucky me, I got a little bonus trip along the way.

Chapter 9

Forgiveness

If you were to ask me what one thing can heal faster and better than anything else, I would have to say forgiveness—most importantly, the act of forgiving ourselves for anything and everything. I think the most powerful thing that can affect our other lifetimes, if indeed they do exist, is the amount of stuff we hold on to and refuse to forgive before we die.

I read a story in an Edgar Cayce publication a number of years ago that made a huge impact on me. It altered the way I treat clients when past-life issues show up. This particular story was written by a woman who practiced healing work. She took a trip abroad with a group unknown to her at the start. During the trip, an incident occurred where she felt judged by another person on the tour. She didn't know the woman. Just to clarify, I will call the writer of the story Mary and the woman she encountered on the trip Betty. When Mary came home from the trip, she didn't feel safe leaving her home and was unable to practice her healing work on others.

In order to find out the cause of the problem, she went into a meditation where she was shown the story. Here is what I recall. In a past lifetime, Mary appeared as an old woman who worked as a healer. I'll call her Old Mary. The community where she lived thought her work was evil or somehow associated with the devil. Mary saw the townspeople being led by their religious leader to Old Mary's home. The intention of the mob was to stone her to death. Mary watched in horror as Old Mary's best friend (Old Betty) cast the first stone. The odd thing was that Old Betty, in that life, was not only Old Mary's best friend, but she was also a healer who knew and worked with Old Mary. Fearing that she would be recognized as a healer and wanting to avoid the fate of her friend, she threw the stone.

Mary came out of this meditation not knowing what to do at first. She decided she needed to forgive the incident and everyone involved. I recall that it took her several sessions of meditation, but she somehow finally entered the past life and approached her former self, Old Mary. She explained what was about to occur. Mary pleaded, saying that it was of utmost importance not only for her own life but also for many others that she (Old Mary) forgive everyone involved. She admitted to Old Mary that she would not be able to save her but said she would be there with her during the entire event for support, though no one else would be able to see her or know she was present.

At that moment, Mary looked out the window and saw the townspeople approaching, just as she had seen in her meditation. Once they were outside, she saw Old Betty throw the first stone and watched the event unfold until she witnessed the death of Old Mary. Here is the difference. She could actually feel the forgiveness from Old Mary as she passed away. When Mary came out of the meditation, all of her fears of leaving the house and resuming her healing work were gone.

This is my best recollection of the account that I read. What I know for sure is that I use what I learned from this story to be a better practitioner. Now when I work with clients and past-life issues come up, I always do forgiveness work. That is probably the biggest part of the treatment. We forgive all others who have hurt us and our loved ones and forgive ourselves for hurting others and for any and all hurt we have caused ourselves.

I also believe that ancestral issues that show up can be treated with forgiveness. When ancestral issues test positive, I often ask to find out how many generations ago the problem began. I used to test to find out what the story was, but that takes far too long and is usually not important to clear the issue. There are times when we do need to know, but it's not often. (It's interesting, yes, but important? No.)

Usually clients have no knowledge of the relative, but they often see the trait in other relatives on that side of the family. For example, if there is an overwhelming sense of neediness in the client and it shows up as an ancestral issue on the mother's side, there might be a sense of neediness that his or her mother, siblings, or maternal aunt, uncle, grandparent, etc., also has. Sometimes when I am clearing the client of that energy, I start to get a feeling of what happened to the original individual.

To help you understand, I'll give an example of what I mean. Perhaps somewhere down the line, the ancestor was abandoned. He or she experienced tremendous fear and died alone. This energy of needing to be near others or needing help, whatever the need is, stayed stuck on this plane. I believe that the energy does not die with the person, so on some level, it needs to be released. Now, how does the energy transfer to another ancestor, especially if the two individuals have not had direct contact? I have no clue. Perhaps it's just in the energetic field of an individual. Maybe one of the great scientific minds understands this and can explain it. If not today, then maybe one day it will be known. All I know at this moment is that when we do the work and free the energy, the clients usually have a beneficial result.

When I was a less-experienced practitioner, I had a client who came to me with a condition of lymphedema, which was the result of having a mastectomy. She'd had breast cancer, had been treated, and was cancer free. I congratulated her on being a cancer survivor. She glared at me and practically shouted, "I am not a cancer survivor! I am a cancer victim!" Yikes! I couldn't believe the amount of anger she was carrying. I felt in my heart that she needed to do a lot of forgiveness work, but I was too apprehensive to tell her that. At that time, I didn't understand the importance of forgiveness, as I do now. I didn't think she would be open to the idea, so at first, I didn't say anything. We worked together for a few sessions. As we talked, she told me about her family and how she hated some of them. She loved her husband, children, and grandchildren but loathed her mother and sisters. Apparently, while growing up, she had been her father's favorite, and ever since his death, she had not gotten the love and attention that she craved from the family she was born into. I finally got the courage to speak up about forgiveness as something inside of me urged me to do so. I had a strong feeling that her life depended on it. I clearly recall the day I suggested forgiving her family. I tiptoed around the idea to be as gentle as possible so as not to upset her.

She screamed, "Forgive them? I will never forgive them! They don't deserve my forgiveness! I would rather die first; then they'll be sorry!"

I was speechless. I attempted to explain that by forgiveness, I didn't mean condoning their bad behavior and the hurt they had caused her. I meant releasing her from the emotional charge of the pain. That was what was important. When we are angry and blame others, it doesn't affect them as much as it affects us. And forgiveness doesn't mean that we should continue to be hurt or abused. It only means to release and let go so that *we* do not continue to suffer. But she chose to hang on to her anger and victimhood.

Within a few weeks, she told me she had been diagnosed with liver cancer, and though she went through treatment with chemotherapy and radiation, she eventually passed away. It saddened me tremendously, but there was nothing I could do to help her. Can I say for sure that if she had chosen to forgive, she never would have had liver cancer? Of course not. There is no way to prove the two were connected. Is it a possibility? Maybe. Would she have lived a more peaceful life in the meantime? Probably. We all make our own choices as far as our thinking goes. I often ask myself, *Would I rather be right, or would I rather be happy?* There was a time when I wanted to be right. These days, I'd rather be happy.

I would like to mention here that in Chinese medicine, each organ in the body is affected by a particular emotion. The liver is connected to the emotion of anger. If you were wondering about the others, here is a quick list:

heart: joy or lack of joy
lungs: grief and sadness
stomach: worry or being over sympathetic
spleen and pancreas: low self-esteem
kidneys and bladder: fear and paralyzed will
liver and gallbladder: anger and resentment
large intestine (colon): stubbornness and unwillingness to let go
small intestine: inability to make decisions

This is a brief and incomplete description that is highly simplified. Traditional Chinese medicine (TCM) has a deep and profound understanding regarding the organs of the body and their functions that goes far deeper than the Western medical model.

Chapter 10

Forgiveness, Part 2

I feel it is important to add this chapter with a thought that could assist in healing the planet on an energetic level. But first, here is a bit of personal information. I am part Armenian. (Actually, I am Armeno-Rican. My father was born in Puerto Rico, and my mother was Armenian.) My mother was born as my grandparents fled from the old country during the Armenian genocide in 1923.

One night, I attended a screening of a documentary called *My Mother's Voice*, which is based on the book by my friend Kay Mouradian, EdD. The movie tells the story of her mother's survival during the Armenian genocide. A discussion followed, which was led by two authors, Professor Donald Miller of USC and his wife, Lorna Touryan Miller. Mrs. Miller is the child of Armenian genocide survivors. Together they have written a couple of books called *Survivors: An Oral History of the Armenian Genocide* (1993) and *Armenia: Portraits of Survival and Hope* (2003). They have also conducted extensive interviews with female survivors of the 1994 Rwanda genocide.

After viewing the movie, which reveals many horrific atrocities, Lorna Miller told the audience, "Imagine what it must have felt like to . . ." and then, in descriptive language, voiced many awful scenarios that many Armenian women experienced during the genocide.

At that point, I did the best I could to protect myself from those visions. I crossed my arms over my chest to protect my solar-plexus chakra.* Then I turned my thoughts to something completely different while she led the audience in this exercise.

I didn't react this way to pretend none of it ever happened. It is important work to acknowledge the truth of what happened to so many. But by the same token, I have learned and practiced manifestation techniques for many years, and I manifest things quickly. I was taught back in the late 1980s while studying the Science Of Mind that the more you practice conscious manifesting, the faster the manifestations will appear. I was warned, "You had better watch what you think about, because it comes about quickly." The skeptic in me didn't understand how that could be, and I didn't really believe it. But as it turns out, it's true. I try to be as aware and as conscious of my thoughts as possible, but I still find myself, at times, dwelling on things other than what I desire to be, to have, and to do. When we focus on thoughts, we are bringing them into our consciousness, and the creative force of the universe begins to bring those realities about into our physical world. Not every thought becomes a manifested reality. It depends on the amount of time and the intensity of emotion used while contemplating. And I don't mean to imply that my listening to the discussion would have brought about another genocide. But on some level, I knew that focusing on those thoughts might bring a less-than-peaceful experience into my own life in some way. I'll talk more about that in the chapter "Things You Can Do."

I left the event feeling conflicted. Focusing on the horrors of the past doesn't help people heal. I have a few Armenian friends who still harbor much anger and resentment toward the Turkish people. They themselves did not personally suffer back then, but it seems as though they suffer today thinking about the past. The individuals who caused the suffering back then are most likely not still living, yet children of survivors are in pain. In fact, the couple who led the discussion spoke about the generations following a genocide that continue to be affected.

The movie was based on the story of Flora. I knew her as Filor. My grandmother was a good friend of hers. In 1992, I asked my grandmother, at the age of ninety-one, just before she passed away, to tell me what she remembered about the genocide. She thought for a brief moment and then opened her mouth to speak, but instead of words, I heard sobbing. Her body shook as she rocked back and forth. The only words that she could utter were "I can't . . . I can't."

Throughout my life, I heard stories about the genocide, but never from my grandparents. Not one hostile or angry word was ever spoken regarding the event. My mother shared a few bits of information she had heard about how my grandfather was taken prisoner at the time. He was a clever tailor and had sewn pieces of gold into the lining of his clothing. When he was taken away, he pulled some of the gold out and bribed his Turkish captors. He told them he had access to a lot of gold and if they let him go, he would lead them to it. Then, somehow, he made his escape.

My point is that harboring anger is not healthy. I am not suggesting that we sweep the whole event under the rug either. In order to heal the past, we must confront it—look it square in the eye and deal with the pain. Once we acknowledge it, we can process it and clear it. Trying to hold on to make *them* wrong is not the answer. We must be willing to give up our story altogether. Again, I don't mean we should ignore it, but it's best released to be history. Realize that it's no longer the present but the past.

Though I am using this experience as an example, I feel it is as important to release and forgive anything that continues to be a thorn in our side, whether it's something as huge as war or the smallest petty issue that we just can't get over. Holding on to it creates an energetic disturbance on some level.

Let me give you an analogy to clarify my point. If you had a dirty, infected wound and you kept picking at it and poking it, you would continually irritate it without allowing it to heal. On the other hand, if you were to cover it up and just try to ignore it, hoping it would go away, it would most likely fester and become a bigger problem in the long run. We need to address the wound. We must look at it and analyze what needs to be done to get rid of the pain and infection, and *then* it can heal.

I wish I had known then what I know now. To watch my grandmother cry her eyes out was extremely painful for me. I felt helpless. Now I have tools and techniques. (For those of you who need immediate help, I suggest Gary Craig's website, www.emofree.com. This is a simple yet amazingly powerful technique you can learn to work on yourself to release the emotional pain of any situation.)

My grandmother was one of the kindest, gentlest souls I have ever met. I don't recall ever hearing her utter an unkind word about anyone. She might not have been able to release her past memories, but she forgave the perpetrators. My grandfather died when I was about nine. He was also one of the kindest people I have ever known. I remember him smiling and laughing, constantly pulling practical jokes. One would never have known that he'd suffered the heinous treatment he had experienced. Because of their forgiveness, I didn't grow up with hate and anger. Their forgiveness was one of the greatest gifts they gave me. I don't know if it was even a conscious decision they made. It was never discussed.

Forgiveness never means condoning awful behavior. It means acknowledging that it happened and letting it go in order to move beyond it. My response to the question "How do you forgive?" is to begin with the willingness to do so. Then say the words. At first, you might not believe the words you're saying, but continue. Eventually, you will get there.

Chapter 11

Spirit Speaks

I have said that I hear a voice or voices. That's not really accurate. I would call them "thought forms." To describe it best, let me put it this way: think of a memory. Do you hear the memory or see the memory? No. This is how it is when I get my information. I have absolutely no idea who or what brings it to me. Is it God? My angels? My higher self? My subconscious mind? There is no way for me to know, but I have learned to trust it.

I used to argue with it. Before I was an intern in Oriental medical school, I was an observer. We were told to watch the interaction of the patients with the interns and be as inconspicuous as possible. We were not to say a word or participate in any way.

So there I was, standing quietly in the corner of a treatment room with two interns and a patient. I'm good at following rules—at least, I used to be. The patient was in pain and could not stand to be touched at all. Even swiping her skin gently with an alcohol swab caused her to scream. The two interns were frantic, trying to figure out how they were going to needle her when they couldn't even make contact with the lightest touch. It was then that I had a strong urge to kneel down and hold her feet.

But I was a good observer, and I resisted the temptation. The voice was directing me more forcefully now to hold the soles of her feet. In my mind, I said, *No, I'm not allowed to touch her.* But the voice persisted. I argued with the feeling that was overwhelming me. Now I was getting ticked off. *Stop it,* I thought. *I am not going to touch her. I'm not allowed, so leave me alone.*

Here's what I learned. When you argue with the voice, it wins. Suddenly, I became nauseated. The voice directed me with greater intensity to hold her feet. Throwing up is not one of my favorite pastimes. The feeling of nausea overrode the embarrassment of speaking up.

"Excuse me," I murmured. "May I touch your feet?" Everyone stared at me for a moment, so I continued. "I think it may help." I assured the patient I would barely touch them and would immediately stop if it was in any way painful.

The woman said, "Go ahead and try it since nothing else is working."

I gently put my hands on the soles of her feet, and I took long, slow breaths. Of course, I had no clue what I was doing or why I was doing it, but as suddenly as it had appeared, my nausea was gone. Then I heard the woman say, "Okay. You can go ahead and stick the needles in me."

"Are you sure?" one of the interns asked incredulously.

"As long as she's holding my feet, I'm fine," she replied as she relaxed back in the chair. (Though we usually had patients on tables, she was sitting on a chair. Lying down was much too uncomfortable for her.)

I held her feet for the duration of the treatment. After she left, I heard the two interns discussing between themselves how touching the feet must have anchored the chi to lower the degree of liver-yang rising or whatever explanation they were cooking up. Our ego mind seems to always need a logical explanation. What was the mechanism of operation involved? Though I'll never know the answer to that question, I learned that when Spirit speaks, it's important to listen. And when I don't, Spirit has ways of making me pay attention.

Sometimes Spirit comes up with the most outlandish suggestions. That is when I truly know I'm working out in left field. Here is an example of that. I was treating a young boy for allergies, when his mother mentioned that she had lost a baby ten years earlier. She admitted to me that not a day went by that she didn't mourn for the little one. I was primarily using the Emotional Freedom Techniques modality for trauma cases during that time and suggested we try that to relieve her emotional pain. The long version of that process involves tapping on certain acupuncture points and then counting and humming a song while continuing to tap on one particular point.

My usual choices for people to hum were simple songs, including "Happy Birthday," "Twinkle, Twinkle, Little Star," "Mary Had a Little Lamb," and the like. As we progressed in the tapping protocol, I realized I couldn't ask her to hum any of those in this situation. It seemed too cruel. I turned to Spirit and silently requested, *Give me a song for her to hum.* The answer I received was "In-A-Gadda-Da-Vida," and I thought, *Are you kidding me? The song by Iron Butterfly? No way. I will* not *ask her to hum that.* I said, *Give me another song*, but I heard the same answer. As we progressed with the tapping, I was quickly approaching the point where I needed her to hum. Because I was running out of time, I was more forceful, and I mentally demanded to be given another song for her to hum.

This time, the answer was different. I heard, *Tell her to hum her husband's favorite song.* I telepathically sent my thanks for something I could finally use. I asked my client, "What's your husband's favorite song?"

She replied, "Oh, it's 'In-A-Gadda-Da-Vida.'"

I burst out laughing, which I knew was completely inappropriate under the circumstances, but I couldn't help myself. I quickly apologized and explained the entire scenario that had been going on in my head. She was one of the few people I trusted to understand my weirdness at that time, so I felt safe and comfortable explaining the mental dialogue. She began to laugh as well. Once we pulled ourselves together, I tested her without continuing the protocol because I had felt a big shift in her energy field. Sure enough, the emotional charge was gone. She agreed the emotional pain had lifted, and I never heard her complain of that issue again. When they say laughter is the best medicine, I have to agree. Now I almost never try to argue with or outsmart Spirit. It doesn't seem to work.

Not too long after this, I saw her and her husband together. I wanted to know if she had told him of the experience, but she hadn't. I asked if I could tell him the story, and she allowed me to do so. Here's the kicker: when I mentioned the song "In-A-Gadda-Da-Vida," her husband replied, "That's not my favorite song."

Another case involved the use of a crystal. I have lots of crystals, and I occasionally use them in my treatments. I've taken classes in crystal use and have read books on them, but I don't have the affinity for them that many other energy workers do. This next session taught me the power of using crystals.

Sam was a born healer, though he never charged for his healing work. He made his living building sets in Hollywood. He said he could touch someone and the person would be healed. He never knew how it happened. It just did. Sam never studied or read about healing. He was born with the gift. How cool is that? But he had lost his abilities. He didn't know why or what had happened. The gift was just gone.

Sam was one of the most humble, unassuming, quiet people I've met. There was a calm and peace that radiated from his being. He came to see me because someone had suggested I might be able to restore his healing abilities. He explained his situation and asked if I could help him. I confessed, "I have no idea." He told me he liked my answer because he had been to many healers who had all promised him the world but had done nothing for him. At least he appreciated my honesty.

So there he was on my table. At the time, the only thing I knew to try was Reiki. As he lay there, he asked me, "Do you know your table is broken? The right side is an inch or two lower than the left side."

"Really?" I responded. I knew there was nothing wrong with my table. It was practically new and in perfect condition, but I was not going to argue with him. I put my hands on Sam and allowed the energy to flow through me. Then a clear thought-form-like voice said, *Get the kyanite.* I have a beautiful specimen of blue kyanite, which I kept in another room at the time.

Now, this was before I learned my lesson of not arguing with the voice, so I mentally said, *No. I don't leave my people once I've started working on them.*

But the voice repeated, *Get the kyanite.*

No, I stubbornly replied, *I've already started working on him.*

Then the voice startled me as it seemed to yell at me, *Get the kyanite!*

Okay, I'll get it, I silently relented. I excused myself and told Sam I would be right back. I found the rock and asked him if he would mind holding it in his hand while I worked.

After holding it about one minute, he said, "How strange. Your table just fixed itself."

"Well, that's good," I said. What can you really say in a situation like that?

Then he added, "And now the right half of my body is touching the left half of my body."

So I asked him, "How long have you been separated?"

He responded, "My whole life. This is the first time I'm together." (And people think I'm weird.)

So my rock was able to connect Sam's parts, but unfortunately, I was not able to assist in restoring his healing abilities. And believe me, I would have loved to have done that. The impression that I got with Sam when he left was a feeling that his right arm (his healing arm) was clogged up with darkness. Back then, I didn't have the knowledge or skills that I have today, so I didn't know to trust that hunch. I have since learned that clearing the congested energy is vitally important.

I finally learned to listen, and when I do, it pays off. I think it even saved my life on one occasion. Several years ago, I heard about a class I wanted to attend up in Sacramento. It was an all-day class on a Sunday, and I decided it would be a good idea to go. It was so long ago that I can't even remember what it was. As it turned out, the class wasn't worth my time, but the experience of getting there was priceless.

I pondered how to get there from Los Angeles. I considered flying, but I soon had an ominous feeling about the trip. I didn't know why. It could have been whatever speaks to me telling me not to go, but I wasn't able to interpret the meaning clearly. The only thing I knew for sure was that with this bad feeling, I was not going to risk my life as a possible plane-crash victim.

I spoke to a friend about the trip, and he volunteered to drive me. He said if we left at midnight and drove all night, I could sleep in the car and we could be there by the time the class began in the morning. Then he would sleep in the car during the day, and we would drive back Sunday night after the class. He seemed eager to make the trip, so I gratefully agreed.

All was well until we set out on our journey. It was midnight. He was driving my car, and I settled in to sleep, but I couldn't. I had a bad feeling come over me that I couldn't explain. So I began to pray. I prayed for a safe trip. I prayed for the road to be clear and safe. I prayed for all the other drivers on the road. I put a white light around the car. I put a gold light around the white light around the car. I continued to pray for several hours, but still, the feeling that something bad was to occur would not lift. Finally, around four o'clock in the morning, having been awake and praying constantly, I was exhausted, and even though I didn't feel safe, I closed my eyes and began to drift off into sleep.

I awakened when I heard a song in my head that I hadn't heard since I was a child. The song invoked the memory of my mother playing records at night in my bedroom as my sisters and I drifted off to sleep. Some were teaching records, such as phonetics; some were nursery rhymes; and some were lullabies.

The song that I heard as we drove was "Angels Watching over Me." As I listened, I recalled that that particular song was not one of my favorites, so I mentally ejected that song out of my head and substituted another song. As I relaxed to listen to the song of my choice, the first song popped right back in. I popped it out again and began to replay *my* choice. Once again, "Angels Watching over Me" began in my head. I continued to fight it (I mentioned I was stubborn, right?) until I thought, *What the heck, I'll go ahead and listen to that one.* Then I drifted off to sleep.

I woke up and heard my friend cry out, "Oh no!" as we began to skid off the road.

A calm, soothing voice within me said, "Keep your eyes closed and you will be fine."

Okay, I thought, *I can do that.* I kept my eyes closed and began to silently repeat, *We are protected. God is here. We are safe. All is well,* and words to that effect. I had a strong sense of knowing that the car was going to start rolling, so I braced myself and waited for it to begin. Instead of rolling, however, we began to spin. I was quite surprised, because that was completely contrary to what I knew was to take place. The spinning sensation finally stopped, and we were at a standstill.

I paused a couple of beats and opened my eyes. The car was in a ditch. We were unharmed, without a scratch on either of us, though the car did sustain some damage. The front bumper was gone, and there was some other front-end damage, but inside the car, we were safe. The airbags didn't even deploy.

My friend took off, looking for help. This was before everyone carried a cell phone. We were in a fairly remote area, but we could see some sort of a building or service station down the road. It was five o'clock in the morning. While he was gone, the California Highway Patrol showed up and asked me what had happened. I told them I had fallen asleep and really hadn't seen what had occurred.

Here is where it got strange. The officer explained that our tire tracks were headed straight for a light pole. He said if we had hit it, the pole would have crushed us and the car. He had seen this happen too many times, and there were never any survivors. But he couldn't understand how we had missed the pole, as the tire tracks continued on the other side of the light pole. The other officer handed me his card and said they were going to call a tow truck to pull my car out of the ditch, but they were going to take off because there was no logical explanation that they could write up in a report. If I needed a report later for insurance purposes, he said to call the number on his card, and they would figure something out to say at that time. Then they left.

When my friend returned, I asked him if he had seen what had happened during the accident. He said he thought he'd drifted off to sleep for a moment, and when he'd opened his eyes, we were heading toward the light pole. "It was the weirdest thing," he whispered incredulously. "Just as we were about to hit the light, it suddenly disappeared." The next thing he knew, we were in the ditch.

The tow truck arrived and pulled us out. The rest of the trip was uneventful. I attended my class, and that evening, we drove back to Los Angeles. I took my car in to get it repaired the next day. That afternoon, the mechanic asked me how I had gotten the car there without a radiator. I told him we had driven it from Sacramento the day before in that condition and had had no problem. He said that was impossible. The radiator was gone.

All I can say is I'm grateful I kept my eyes closed when I was instructed to do so, because I doubt I would have had the faith to believe we would be fine had I seen what there was to see. I'm also glad I didn't know the car was unable to be driven. Do I believe in miracles? Yes!

There have been three occasions in my life when I have really and truly heard a voice from someone who wasn't visible. Most of the time, as I've stated, when I refer to my voices, they are more like thought forms—mental pictures or ideas that impart information—but not in these cases. The first voice I heard was so real that I turned around to see who was speaking to me. It was in the year 1986. I remember clearly because that was a significant year in my life.

I was on a Greyhound bus. I had been visiting a friend in Santa Cruz. It was a Sunday evening, and I was taking the bus to the San Jose airport to catch a flight home to Los Angeles. I could see the airport far in the distance, and I was checking my watch, making sure I would have ample time to board my plane. It was then that a voice right behind me said, "Don't worry. No matter what happens, you'll be fine." I knew he was speaking to me, because he said it directly behind me. I turned around to look at the stranger and ask him why he would say such an odd thing to me. But when I turned to look, there was no one behind me.

I looked at the woman sitting across from me and asked, "Did you hear that voice?"

Apparently, she hadn't. She looked at me as if I were crazy and moved as far away from me as possible. Just then, I noticed that the bus was turning away from the airport. We were moving in the wrong direction, and I had a plane to catch. I ran up to the driver in a panic and asked, "Why aren't we going to the airport? I thought we were headed for the airport! I need to go to the airport!"

He calmly turned to me and responded, "We don't go there anymore on Sundays."

"What!" I exclaimed. "I have a flight to catch. What do I do?" I must mention that I had led a sheltered life up to that point and had no idea how to get home. I couldn't have felt more lost and confused had I been dropped off in a foreign country, unable to communicate with the natives. I know it sounds ridiculous, but that was truly how I felt about my situation.

The bus driver said, "Just get off in Hayward and take BART to the Oakland airport. You can catch a flight from there."

I was deer-in-the-headlights paralyzed with fear. I didn't know what a BART was or how to get to the Oakland airport. I was absolutely terrified. When we arrived in Hayward, the bus driver

called to me, "You can get off here." He pointed me to what he called
BART, and I got off the bus. As he drove away, I just stood there, not
knowing what to think or do.

Suddenly, a man appeared next to me. I don't know where he
came from. He said to me, "Are you looking for BART? I'll walk with
you." So I followed him. He asked me if I was looking to get to the
airport, and I nodded. Turns out BART is the metro system. Who
knew? I'm sure lots of people, but until then, I wasn't one of them.
Anyway, he helped me buy a ticket, and we set off for the airport.
I didn't say much to him, though he tried to put me at ease. He
mentioned he had a daughter about my age, and if she had been lost
and alone, he hoped a stranger would help her out, so he wanted to
do that for me.

I happened to be wearing an Angels jacket from the baseball team.
There were some unsavory characters on the train, and they were
laughing at my jacket and joking about angels. My new friend began
to kindly interact with them, and I noticed they quickly changed their
attitude and left me alone after that. I was still feeling apprehensive
about this entire situation, but I was comforted that I had someone
helping me and looking out for me. Interestingly, I felt safe with this
stranger, and though it made no sense, he felt vaguely familiar.

We got off the train at the Oakland airport, and I attempted to
buy a ticket home, but there were no flights until the next morning. I
was going to school in Los Angeles and had a test the next morning
that I didn't want to miss. I was in a quandary as to what to do
next. The gentleman suggested I take BART to the airport in San
Francisco. He said he was sure there was a red-eye to LAX that I
could catch, so we each bought another ticket to take BART to San
Francisco. I felt guilty that this man was going out of his way on my
behalf, but he insisted that it was on his way and no trouble at all.
When we arrived at the airport, he wanted to accompany me, but I
insisted he had helped me enough and I would be fine. I asked him
for his name, phone number, and address, which he gave me.

Indeed there was a red-eye flight to LAX, and I arrived safely. A couple of days later, I attempted to call the gentleman to thank him and tell him I was sending him a gift to let him know how much I appreciated his kindness. As it turned out, there was no such number. It was disconnected. When I researched his address, it didn't seem to exist. I tried everything I could to locate this kind man. I could never find a trace that anyone with his name existed. That was when I got the chills. I thought about the voice I had heard, and I remembered the Angels jacket I had been wearing. Just as the voice had said while on the bus, everything had been fine. To this day, I wonder if I had an actual angel encounter. It could have been just a big coincidence, but then again . . .

The second time I heard a voice, I was walking out the front door of my parents' home. A voice asked, "What would it be like if one of your parents was gone?"

I looked around to see where the voice had come from. It wasn't a booming sound from the sky but a soft and gentle yet distinct voice. My first thought was *Who said that?* followed by *Why would you say "one of your parents"?* It was obvious to me my father would go first. My mother appeared to be in good health, and my father was ailing. At that time, he was terminally ill and attached to an oxygen tank. He was also eleven years older than my mother. I didn't know what to think of the voice, so I didn't think about it at all—not until my mother suddenly passed on about a week later. There was no warning at all—except for the voice.

My father, an intuitive man, believed my mother communicated with him following her funeral service. He heard her say we could call on her for help anytime we needed it. She informed him that there were rules and that she wouldn't always be allowed to come to our aid. Nevertheless, if we were ever in need, we should always ask.

The next time I heard a voice was later that year. It was a few months following my mother's passing. One night, around two in the morning, I was awake in bed and unable to get to sleep. With my father ill, my uncle recuperating from open-heart surgery, my grandmother nearly ninety and needing assistance, and my sister with Down syndrome living at home needing care, I was a mess attempting to take care of everyone. At the same time, I was working to keep my grades up in school. I felt as though I were going to have a nervous breakdown, and I couldn't handle it anymore. I called out to my mother, not knowing what else to do. "Mom, if you are really there and can help me, then do something. I can't cope any longer," I cried.

At that moment, she appeared in my room. I can't say I saw her with my eyes, but I was aware of her presence. I felt her essence in the room. I could tell you exactly where she was standing. I definitely heard her voice. Clearly, she said, "Turn on the radio." Of all the things she might have said, that was not what I had been expecting. So what could I do? I turned on the radio. She was still in my room, and the radio was on, but there was no sound. I waited in silence for maybe ten minutes. I waited and waited for any sound from the radio. Okay. It was probably only ten seconds, but silence for even that long is unusual over the airwaves. Then I heard a song begin. The lyrics gave me her message. They said something to the effect of "You knew we wouldn't always be together, but we will be again someday. You must go on with your life one day at a time. It will all work out for the best. Just keep moving one day at a time." Of course, those were not the actual lyrics, but that was the message. I knew without a doubt I had made contact with her, and I couldn't give up on life. She came to my rescue two more times after that night. On both occasions, I needed help. I called out to her on one occasion, and the next time, she just appeared unexpectedly and told me what to do when I was in need of assistance.

Spirits also speak through others on our behalf. More than once, I've visited mediums who have given me readings. Shortly before my grandmother passed, she was in a convalescent home, recovering from a broken shoulder and hip. I was expecting her to move back home, and I wanted to surprise her. I had beautiful new wallpaper put up, and I removed the old carpet and refinished the wood floor. I wanted everything to be fresh and new for her arrival home. Unfortunately, she passed on the morning the painter showed up to finish painting the trim. I felt incredible sorrow upon her death. I hadn't told her that I was redoing her room, because I had wanted to surprise her.

It was possibly over a year after she was gone before I saw one of the mediums, but imagine my surprise when the medium laughed and said to me, "I have a message from your grandmother. I'm quoting her exactly, and it's not proper English," she continued, "but she says, 'Thank you for making pretty in my room.'" (My grandmother was Armenian and spoke broken English with a prominent accent.) Apparently, she had gotten to see her new room after all.

Years later, I went to see another medium. He asked me who had a birthday coming up in two weeks. He paused. "Or did they just have a birthday two weeks ago?" he asked. "Something about a birthday and two weeks."

My birthday was going to be in two weeks to the day. This man had no information about me prior to the reading. He didn't even know my whole name. He said he saw a man and a woman he believed were my father and mother holding a birthday cake together, and they were placing it on my lap. One point for him.

He soon scored a second point. On the way to that appointment, I had thought about a voice teacher I had studied with, Margaret Keane, who had died a few years before. During the reading, the medium said to me, "There's another woman here," and he described Margaret to a tee. I said I knew who she was and was surprised she had shown up. He then said, "She's telling me that you invited her to be here." She had been a good friend to me as well as a teacher. All I had done was think of her for a moment as I drove to the appointment, but I guess that was enough to be considered an invitation.

I've been told that the moment we think of someone who has gone to the other side, he or she immediately gets the call and is here for us. Though we might not be able to detect his or her presence, I wouldn't be at all surprised if that's the truth. It certainly seemed to be so in this case.

I've heard more stories than I can count regarding communicating with loved ones who have passed. Many years ago, I received a phone call around midnight from my friend Helen, who apologized for calling so late. She said this was important. Her mother's friend had passed away earlier that evening, and the woman had appeared to Helen after her death. She had sat on Helen's bed, and they'd had a long chat. Helen told me what they had talked about at length. She said she'd needed to call me immediately because the woman had just left and if she had waited to tell me about it in the morning, she would have thought it was just a dream. Helen wanted me to know that it had actually happened and that there was no question about it. She knew of all people, I would believe her, and it was important that she tell someone. I was excited, because Helen is one of the biggest skeptics I know. At the time, she believed if you couldn't touch it, measure it, or quantify it, then it didn't exist. She is extremely bright and scientific minded in her approach to everything. But she knew this was a real experience.

Fearing that by morning she would rethink the experience and dismiss it as a dream, she needed to express it to someone. I assured her that once someone experiences something like this, there is no going back. You know it's the truth, and you are a changed person. I figured since she knew without a doubt it was real, she would no longer question the memory. We ended the call, and I went to sleep.

The next morning, I called her. I wanted to talk further about her experience the night before. "What experience?" she asked.

I thought she was kidding and said, "The spirit. You know, your mother's friend who had the long visit with you last night."

"Oh, that. I think I must have been dreaming. Or I was making it up. I'm sorry I called you. I'm sure nothing happened. I don't know what I was thinking." She completely dismissed the whole event. I couldn't believe it. I had never heard of anyone experiencing what she had and later denying that it happened. I believe her religious beliefs are meaningful to her, and this experience might not have been in alignment with her faith.

What I do know is that I was wrong about believing that it would change her viewpoint. From that occurrence, I learned that we all have our own path to follow. Helen's path might not be anything close to my path, but it is the perfect path for her. Maybe believing that spirits can communicate would rock the foundations of her beliefs too much. It's not my business to figure it out or to try to convince her otherwise.

After I wrote this story down, I contacted Helen to make sure I had her permission to include her story in this book. She agreed and told me she'd had another happening with the spirit world. I guess she has changed her viewpoint after all.

In her own words, this is Helen's story:

> The incident at my aunt and uncle's house immediately after Uncle Tommy died is much more difficult to deny for two reasons. It happened during daylight, and I was wide awake at the time, and it did not involve a visitation in the sense of actually perceiving the presence visually. I just asked him in desperation for immediate help and information.
>
> Uncle Tommy often told me that when he died, he wanted to be buried in his navy uniform. He would become adamant about it and said that I was the only one he could count on. He said, "She"—meaning my aunt—"can't be bothered with it, so I am counting on you to make sure I am buried in my navy uniform." So over and over again, I would solemnly promise to carry out his wishes. The day after Uncle Tommy passed away, my aunt and my mother went to make arrangements. I met them after work at my aunt and uncle's house, and they were all in a panic. My aunt did think about the uniform. She, my mother, and two caregivers had just spent three hours combing the house for the uniform, and nothing had turned up.
>
> They retired to the den, thinking the situation hopeless, and I asked my aunt if she would allow me to

have a look around. She said to go ahead, but they had already covered all the ground there was.

I went into their bedroom and opened up their closets but found nothing but everyday clothing and suits and dresses. In desperation, I actually started talking to my uncle and said something like the following: "Look, Uncle Tommy *you* made me promise that I would make sure you were buried in your uniform, but you never told me where the damn thing was. If I am to honor this promise, you are going to have to tell me where the hell it is! I can't keep my promise to you if you don't help me, so help me! Please!"

This was not my house and not my stuff and was totally strange, and I just did not know where to even continue looking. I stepped into the hallway to think out a strategy and noticed the cedar closet. I knew that this was where the safe was and probably dress coats and jackets. When I was staying with them for a few months after my aunt broke her hip, Uncle Tommy was always drumming it into me to never, ever under any circumstances open that closet. Because the safe was in there, it was connected to the burglar alarm, and if I opened it while the alarm was engaged, I would set it off. This, of course, was followed by a detailed description of a nightmare scene involving the police, dogs, and a SWAT team. I, of course, would say, "Yeah, yeah, I get it already. Don't worry. I will never in my life open this door."

So at that moment, I sort of felt a kind of perverse joy, just like a kid who is doing something he knows he is not supposed to. I said, "Uncle Tommy, the alarm isn't even on, and I am going to open this freakin' door." Sure enough, there was the safe and a bunch of dress jackets, coats, and furs. I moved them and found an ancient suitcase in the back. I pulled it out and opened it. On top was a pair of gray men's slacks, then some black slacks, and then a suit jacket. I thought, *Crap!* Underneath the last pair of slacks was a few layers of tissue paper. When

I pulled those back, there was a blue jacket. I lifted it out and saw that it had stripes and insignia, and there was no doubt about it: this was a uniform! Under the jacket were the matching pants.

I did not see an apparition, and I did not hear a voice, but the feeling was such warmth—exciting and peacefully loving at the same time. I just kept saying thank you. And then I did something really weird. I put the jacket on and just sat in the bedroom, wearing and snuggling into the jacket worn so long ago by a navy commander, my uncle, found by opening the forbidden door. There is no way to deny it. I did, in fact, ask a dead man for immediate help and information—and I got it.

I love this story because Helen didn't hear a voice or have a strange apparition show up. She writes, "I stepped into the hallway to think out a strategy and noticed the cedar closet." It was something that drew her attention. That's a powerful way for spirit to speak, but because it seems so mundane, many of us hardly take notice. We are often looking for the booming voice, so we ignore the whisper. I've learned to pay attention to the softest whisper. The thoughts that make no sense or come from left field are often the most meaningful. I used to completely ignore them because they make no logical sense.

I've learned that the logical-sounding thoughts usually come from my ego mind. The odd thoughts come from a place of truth and power. Go figure! One would think it should be the other way around. Start to pay attention to the thoughts that don't make sense, and see how that works for you.

I try to remind my clients that during a session, if they have a weird or unusual thought, to please say it out loud. We can test it to see what it means. There have been plenty of times that I have been unable to find the core issue. Finally, I or the clients will hit upon it, and they tell me, "That's what I kept thinking, but it didn't make sense, so I decided not to mention it." Our problem is that we often edit spirit (or whatever you choose to call it) out of the picture.

Chapter 12

Pets

Many of us have pets that we dearly love. When they are sick or injured, it affects us deeply. When we lose them, it hurts as much as losing a family member—sometimes more so, as I found out while on a vacation.

I was on a cruise ship, sitting next to a lovely woman, and we began to chat about all kinds of things. As we talked about our families, she began to cry. She told me she had lost her little dog a few years back and couldn't get over the grief. She knew it sounded ridiculous, because it had happened over seven years ago, but whenever she thought about her dog, she couldn't help it: she began to sob. Her dog was the only being that had given her unconditional love. Sheepishly, she admitted she loved that dog even more than her own children.

As she spoke, I could feel the overwhelming sense of sadness, and I just had to do something to help her. If there was a way to relieve her grief in just a few minutes, I asked, would she be willing to try?

"Well, that's just impossible," she said through tears. "I've tried everything, even therapy, and nothing works. I'll grieve until the day I die."

Being the stubborn Capricorn that I am, I persisted. "What if there was a way that you were unfamiliar with?" I asked. "Would you at least be willing to give it a shot? You have nothing to lose."

She finally agreed to give it a try. I had her run through the Emotional Freedom Techniques* protocol. We tapped on certain acupuncture points as she spoke of the sadness, hurt, and pain of the loss of her pet. When we had run through a couple of rounds, which took less than ten minutes, I asked her to tell me about her dog.

She began to relate funny stories and shared some of the things he had done that touched her heart. Now she was smiling, and not a tear was shed. She didn't seem to be aware of this fact as she enthusiastically continued with more dog tales. She was completely oblivious to the change that had happened. I finally interrupted her by asking, "Do you notice that you aren't crying?"

She hesitated and looked around as she seemed to search her mind for something. "Well, isn't that something? I don't feel sad anymore. Not only that, but I don't have the lump in my throat that I always feel when I think of him." She thanked me, and I could sense her joy. Her parting words to me as she walked away were "This is good stuff. You should charge for this."

Here is another story of overcoming the grief of the loss of a pet, directly from the individual herself.

> My experience of healing work with Hoberleigh could be described as a path to discovery. I had recently lost a beloved animal who had suffered from a lifelong illness. The last six months of her life became increasingly difficult, and in her final weeks, I had to accept that though she had fought so hard on many occasions and won, she was too sick to recover this time. I loved her dearly and admired her fortitude. I felt that this animal was a great teacher, and I had learned a great many things from her. I opted to have her put down in our home after she had been unable to eat or drink for many days. I knew it was the best option we had, but I felt so sad and guilty afterward.

Not long after losing Margie, I saw Hoberleigh. She offered to help, and she performed healing work for me. She conducted a series of what I can best describe as simple tests to explore the mind, body, heart, and spirit. Sometimes we don't have the answers we are looking for in our consciousness, but they can be accessed through our spirit. She asked me to make a fist and hold my arm out fully extended. Then she asked me questions about the sadness I felt concerning Margie. There did not seem to be any right or wrong answers, and as she evaluated, she would press firmly down on my outstretched fist. Sometimes I was unable to hold my arm out, and other times, I was easily capable of holding strong against the downward pressure she applied to my arm. Her touch was firm but painless. She felt strongly that there was something more than sadness and asked me aloud what else I might be feeling along with the sadness. When I looked inward, the feeling of guilt came to me. I told her that I felt guilt. She tested again to see if guilt was present. It was, and we explored this new discovery. She worked with me—and, I believe, with Margie—to clear the sadness and guilt. The clearing was emotionally intense at first, and then a subtle sense of calm followed. In the calm state, I felt clear, and we discussed how these strong emotions were linked to a long history of feeling worthless and inadequate in some aspects of my life and trying to compensate with a sort of hypercritical attitude toward myself. I had long sensed this, but in my work with Hoberleigh, I felt a new awareness and clarity regarding this issue.

In the weeks and months that followed, I kept my calm feeling with regard to my Margie and no longer felt the deep pain and sadness of losing her. I was able to contact the good memories of her, including the important lessons I feel she taught me in our time together. However, I began to question this new calm state. I wondered if it was wrong to not feel guilt. I think we often become accustomed to what is comfortable and familiar, even if it is painful or detrimental. The work I have done with Hoberleigh has given me an opportunity to feel what it is to let go of unnecessary guilt and sadness. These emotional states aren't helpful and cause me to miss out on the positive. When I think of Margie now, I think of how I miss her and the beautiful time we had together instead of focusing on the idea that I had failed her in some way. I remember something she did that was endearing or a really good moment that we shared. There were so many good moments, and there is nothing standing in the way of accessing those memories now.

Here are a couple of my own stories regarding my cat Hespia, who is no longer on this earthly plane. She taught me a few things, as did many of my other animals. A number of years ago, she hurt her leg. I was in the kitchen, washing dishes, and I heard a loud *thunk*. I turned around to see what had fallen, and I saw my black cat, Hespia, shoot past me and run out the cat door. In the living room, on the floor, I found a blanket twisted up, and one of my large crystal geodes was on the floor next to the blanket. I've never been able to figure out exactly what happened, but my cat either twisted her leg in the blanket, or maybe the heavy rock landed on it.

When I found her outside, she was limping. Her back left leg was folded up against her body. My first inclination was to take her to the vet, but my voices chimed in. I was told that I could help her and that it would be better this way. I didn't know how badly she was hurt, but there was no blood. She let me gently palpate her leg. Nothing seemed to be broken.

I decided I'd watch her closely and see if I really could help her myself. She moved into one of my closets and chose to stay there. I made a little nest for her there and brought in her food and water. She ended up living in the closet during her convalescence. The only time she crept out was to use the litter box.

On a daily basis, I would crouch next to her, put my hands over her leg, and do some Reiki* work. As I sat there sending the healing energy, my memory of the accident replayed in my mind. I felt guilty, blaming myself and thinking it was my fault. I thought, *I must have put the blanket in a bad spot*, or *Why didn't I leave the crystal on the floor instead of the shelf?* I was constantly focusing on negative thoughts, berating myself for causing her injury. I would tell Hespia how sorry I was for causing the accident. Every day as I worked on her, I worried and blamed myself, and the guilt continued.

After a couple of weeks, I heard another voice. It said, "This guilt isn't helping her. You have to stop that." It was a wake-up call. I thought about it and realized what I was doing. I have had years of training in the Science of Mind. I knew better, but I didn't act like I did. In that moment, I changed my thoughts. I recognized the power of Source. I turned inward, and I used my connection to Creator to command a perfect healing. I began to talk to my cat differently, and I told her that her leg was healing. I said it would now heal faster than it had been, and she would heal so completely that she wouldn't even have a limp. She would walk and run and jump just as she had in the past.

Now, here is an interesting coincidence. Up to that time, she had stayed in that closet except for limping out to use the litter box. The next day, she came out of the closet and began to put weight on her leg. At first, I could see her walking gingerly, but within a couple of days, she walked around the house more, going into the closet only for short periods of time.

A couple of days later, I muscle tested a surrogate* for my cat. The information I got was that she had torn a ligament. I used the surrogate to do another protocol called BodyTalk* for my cat. After fifteen or twenty minutes of treatment, I tested and got the answer that we were done. The healing was complete. From that time on, Hespia no longer limped.

There is one other Hespia story I would like to share. Toward the end of her life, she was sick with cancer in her front paw, and

I was unable to help her. I called another practitioner to work on my cat. Sometimes it is difficult to work on someone you love, because it's impossible to stay neutral. I had been able to work on her before because the situation wasn't life threatening. This time was different.

I scheduled a phone appointment with Marina Rose, my ThetaHealing teacher. She had me sit in the same room with Hespia so that I could observe her during the treatment. I was sitting on my sofa, and Hespia was beside me in a chair. She was sitting up as I spoke with Marina on the phone.

I watched my cat as Marina said, "I'm connecting with your cat now, and I'm going into theta." At that exact moment, I watched my cat trying to keep her eyes open. They kept closing, and she looked as if she were fighting it. Then I saw her body waiver and begin to sink down. She curled up and appeared to be asleep.

Marina was silently doing the healing work. It lasted ten minutes or so, and during that time, I just relaxed and wasn't paying attention to Hespia.

I heard Marina say to me, "I just checked in with your cat, and she's worried about you. She wants you to have the treatment." Now, this was really weird. I glanced over at my cat and saw her standing with her front paws on the arm of the chair, with her eyes wider than I had ever seen. She had a fixed stare directed straight toward me.

I must admit, I was going through personal trauma at that time, having to do with the loss of my twin sister while in the womb. Marina then turned her attention to me, and we worked on that issue.

Chapter 13

My Twin Sister Who Wasn't

There is no proof that I had a twin sister who died in the womb, but I believe it is a possibility. There is no one to ask to confirm anything. My mother has been gone since 1986, and even if she were alive, she might not have known. This story might only make sense to me, but here it is.

Many years ago, I read an article in a chiropractic journal about a man who had a teratoma—a tumor made up of different types of tissue, including skin, hair, muscle, and sometimes even teeth. This gentleman originally went to the doctor complaining of abdominal pain. Nothing was found. He continued to complain, and though nothing was obvious at first, something began to protrude from his abdomen. Over time, the growth began to develop quite rapidly, and it eventually popped out. His M.D. explained that while he was in the womb, he had a twin who didn't make it very far along during the pregnancy, and when it died, his body absorbed it. The reason I remember this story is because he said if it had appeared in the *National Enquirer*, the headlines would have read something like "Man Gives Birth to His Own Twin Brother." That kind of sticks with you—or at least it did me. This is known as the vanishing twin syndrome.

Fast-forward a number of years later. I was having a difficult time in a class I was taking out of town. I became extremely emotional for no apparent reason. In this class, we were learning how to use a Meridian Stress Assessment unit to identify emotional issues. Because I was having such a difficult time, the instructor put me on the machine during a break to determine the cause of my upset. The computer located an issue. The instructor looked at the screen and read out loud, "Vanishing twin syndrome."

In that moment, I burst out in tears. I felt the deepest sense of grief I had ever felt in my life. I heard myself crying out, "She died! She died, and no one even knew she was there. I couldn't help her. She died!"

I tried to stop the tears and the incredible sadness, but I couldn't. My chest felt heavy with pain. The poor woman working on me seemed at a loss. I could tell she hadn't been expecting such an emotional reaction. Neither had I. I don't remember the rest of the class or the following two days of the material presented. This was truly an overwhelming experience. The woman worked on me to relieve the pain, and eventually, I calmed down. I figured that issue was handled. I didn't think of this again for several years.

About eight or ten years later, I began to feel lonely. Though I had lots of friends at the time, I still felt as if something or someone were missing in my life. To tell the truth, I recall feeling as if someone were missing throughout my entire childhood. I never spoke of this, because I just assumed everyone went through life with the exact same feeling. Since no one else ever spoke of it, I thought it was just one of those things no one talked about but everyone felt.

Getting back to the loneliness issue, at some point, I realized my feeling was due to my nonexistent twin sister. Whenever I thought about her, I re-experienced the overwhelming grief. Tears would flow, and I tried everything I could think of to relieve the pain. This went on for months. I have many techniques I use on myself and others to clear emotional pain, but nothing worked in this case. When I wasn't thinking of my twin, life was perfectly fine. Out of the blue, the thought of her would pop into my head, and I would immediately fall apart. I would have to seriously distract myself from the thought of her to carry on. I talked to a few close friends about this, and they assured me she was fine. If she actually did exist in the spirit world, then I knew *she* was fine. Her well-being wasn't my concern. It was me. I was the one who was having the problem. This really didn't make sense to me on any level. I constantly questioned whether this was truly real or some imaginary thought. If it was my imagination, then what caused it? I certainly didn't choose to have these thoughts. But the sorrow was real, and I had to find my way out of this distress somehow.

Try as I might, I couldn't seem to get to the bottom of the problem. Each week, the grief intensified until the breaking point. One day, I dropped something on the floor, and it broke. It was not a big deal, but at that moment, something snapped. I became extremely angry. I rarely lose my temper, and the emotion I felt was out of proportion to the event. I wanted to yell at someone, but I didn't know who. *How dare you treat me like this? Why won't you listen to me? Please listen!* These thoughts kept circulating in my head. I had no clue to whom I was directing these thoughts. I did my best to breathe deeply and let it all go.

A few hours later, when I was peaceful and calm, I was driving quite a distance on a deserted road, and my mind began to wander. I thought to myself, *What was all that about earlier? Who was I mad at?* Immediately, a scene played out in my mind. It seemed like a foggy memory. It was more sound than picture.

I heard my mother's voice saying, "Something's wrong with the baby. I can feel it."

Then a male voice responded, "No, dear, you are fine. I can hear the heartbeat. You are imagining things." Then he chuckled in a patronizing manner. Anger rose in me as I heard the laugh in my head.

I could hear myself trying to communicate to both of them. If I could have spoken, I would have screamed, "She's dying! Help her!

She needs help!" But no one could hear me. Then I was alone, and the grief was overwhelming.

If you're thinking I'd lost my mind, you're not the only one. That's exactly what I was thinking. However, the longer I sat with this vision, the more I realized that it finally all made sense. Now that I possibly knew what was going on, I had something to work on to clear myself. Daily, I worked on releasing the issue. It began to improve, but it didn't completely go away until my cat stepped in and offered up her own session to help me get healed.

To understand that last sentence, you would need to read about my talking cat, Hespia, in the previous chapter. (Just kidding—she never spoke out loud.) I was on the phone with Marina Rose, who was working on Hespia to heal her illness, but Hespia wanted me to get the treatment.

Marina asked me if there was something I needed help healing. I told her I might have had a twin sister who died in the womb, but I wasn't sure. She went into theta* and confirmed my story. As I thought of my sister's death, I became emotional. Using ThetaHealing,* Marina cleared out the trauma from the first month of my fetal life. I recall her working through the first trimester and continually checking in with me as she worked to see how I was feeling.

Once she completed those first three months in the womb, I felt a huge sense of relief. There was just a bit of sadness as I thought of the loss. After she cleared out the fourth month, I was aware of a substantial difference. I stated that it was all gone. I was free of the pain. Marina decided to check it herself using her inner guidance. "No, honey, there's much more in there," I recall her telling me.

She continued through all nine months of the pregnancy. When she finished, I experienced a wonderful shift in my energy. A joyous sense of relief flooded through me. In that moment, all was well. I wasn't sure it would remain that way, but at least I was hopeful that might be the end of that pain.

I'm glad to say that since then, I have not had one bit of grief when thinking of the possibility of having lost a twin. In fact, when all of this was complete, a friend of mine, knowing all that I had gone through with this situation, suggested that I try to communicate with my twin. At first, I thought that sounded ridiculous, but the more I thought about it, the more I considered it. I admit that I don't communicate with her often, but I will share one brief episode. I was on my way into a department store, wanting to buy something to perk up my house. All my taste happens to be in my mouth, so I said (in my mind to my twin), *If you really exist, maybe you can help me. Perhaps you were the one with taste. I'm looking for something that would look nice in my house, so I want you to search around the store and find something, and if it's a good price, then guide me to it.*

As clear as could be, I heard in my head, *Hey, I don't have superpowers.* It was said in a slightly sarcastic yet humorous tone. It made me smile, and I thought to myself, *Yup, you sound like you could be my twin.*

Chapter 14

Ghost Busting

I've mentioned my belief regarding death. When we leave our bodies and move on from the physical plane, our issues stay here in the third dimension. I can't be any more specific, because I really don't know how it all works. My beliefs are based on my experiences, and here is from where much of my belief stems.

I went to India for a month back in 2006. When I came back, I found myself experiencing a roller coaster of emotions. I would break into laughter for no reason and couldn't stop for several minutes. While in India, I went through a process called *Deeksha*. While there, everyone in the program was going through similar experiences, first crying and mourning and then eventually breaking into the laughter phase. I was living in a compound with two hundred women at the time.

My case was slightly different. I stayed in a state of neutrality for the majority of the time. It was in the last few days that things began to shift for me.

There were many dogs on the compound, and they looked to be starving. We were given explicit instructions not to feed them. I have a lot of compassion for animals, and to turn away as they begged for food caused me much grief. It seems to me this was the issue that sparked the beginning of my mourning period. As the days continued, my despair grew to the point of feeling what I can only describe as the sadness of the entire planet. The last couple of days, I found myself on the floor in the fetal position, weeping uncontrollably. Almost everyone there had been through this experience, and they were all now beyond it, but I was stuck smack dab in the middle of it.

My greatest fear at the time was that I would live the rest of my life locked in this mourning phase. Fortunately, it lifted on my last day there. I was back to my old self. I had been hoping to return home as a new-and-improved me, but after what I had gone through, the return of the old me made me happier than I could have ever imagined.

When I returned home, the laughter phase set in. If I hadn't seen the other participants experience it in India, then I would have wondered what was going on. How and why this occurred, I haven't a clue. But I will tell you that while it lasted, it was probably the most fun six months of my life.

Eventually, things changed. I began to feel a sense of loneliness unlike anything I'd ever experienced, including the episode of the missing twin. It was accompanied by a sense of anxiousness in the center of my chest. I would pace back and forth in my living room, saying to no one, "I don't want to be here. I shouldn't be here." This lasted for five years. I wasn't suffering continually. The feeling would just suddenly hit me, and there was nothing I could do to overcome it. I am a great believer in the power of the mind. "Just change your focus," I would tell myself. But I couldn't. Something was stopping me from doing that. I felt as if the Dementors from the *Harry Potter* books had come into my world and sucked the joy out of me. That's the closest and most accurate way to describe what I was feeling.

Each year this sensation attacked me more frequently and lasted longer. I finally got to the point where I thought something was seriously wrong with me. Was I going crazy? When it was not affecting me, I felt like myself again. When it was here, I didn't feel like me.

That's when I began to read *ThetaHealing* by Vianna Stibal. I read about curses, spells, possessions, and wayward spirits—things I had never believed in. One day, as I was talking with a colleague, Tammy, that feeling hit me. It came upon me suddenly, which was unusual because it typically happened when I was alone. I began to pace back and forth, and I said out loud, "I don't want to be here. I shouldn't be here." I said it over and over again. I couldn't stop myself. Then I looked at Tammy and said, "This isn't me."

She looked into my eyes and said, "No, Hoberleigh, you're right. It's not you," and that was when I got it. I had been saying it wasn't me for years, but I didn't hear it until she repeated it back to me. I now knew that it wasn't me but someone else. Tammy asked if she should take me to the emergency room but I declined. Since she had no idea how to help me, she left.

Now that I knew what was going on, I felt I could handle the situation. I read the chapter on releasing spirits, and I put myself in a theta brain wave according to the book. (At this time, I had not yet taken any classes in ThetaHealing.) I went through the process and sent the spirit to the light. From that moment, I felt free. A definite sense of lightness surrounded me. Within a few minutes, I was overcome with an immense feeling of gratitude. It might have been my imagination but it might have been the spirit who was freed. From that moment, the depression I had suffered was gone entirely.

I was free from that feeling for about a year. Then a similar feeling came upon me. This time, I caught it early. I had been working with a woman who had lost some relatives a few years before. As I tested her, I found that some of her issues were tied into the ancestral line. I worked on freeing that energy from her. I called in the ancestors and worked on their energy, releasing them. The session went well, and she verified that much of the emotional weight she had been carrying was gone.

That evening, I wasn't feeling as peaceful as I usually did, but I didn't think much about it. Over the next two days, I was unhappy for no particular reason. On the fourth day, I was miserable. I was visiting some friends, and I could barely stand to be in the same room with other people. I left the room to be alone, wanting to crawl out of my skin because of the emotional discomfort. One of the well meaning women followed me and asked if she could be of help. She sat next to me and gently put her hand on my shoulder.

I had never felt the intensity of anger that overwhelmed me at that moment. In as calm a voice as I could muster, I softly seethed, "Please take your hand off of me." She kept her hand there for a couple of seconds longer. I hate to admit this, because it is so unlike me, but I wanted to slap her across the room. I was shocked at this overwhelming anger that I could barely control. (I don't think she had a clue of the intensity of how I felt in that moment, because she still speaks to me.)

She nodded, got up, and left the room. In that instant, I realized this was not my anger. I didn't know whose it was or what it was about, but I had to release it. Because I am not able to test myself, I had to find a surrogate.* I temporarily joined the others and asked one of my friends to help me test myself. Fortunately, I am blessed with understanding and patient friends. What I found was indeed what I had suspected: another hitchhiker was invading my space. I used the ThetaHealing technique that I had learned from Vianna Stibal's book to release the energy (spirit, entity, soul, being), and immediately, I felt peaceful.

I learned that cutting cords* and clearing myself after working on others is more important than I had thought. I've had to learn that lesson the hard way on more than one occasion.

Chapter 15

Allergies

I will be referring to allergies as sensitivities. All allergies are sensitivities with obvious physical symptoms. Some people have sensitivities that are so mild that they are not even aware that the sensitivities exist. The body, unfortunately, is aware and is weakened to some degree. The cause might not be obvious, so the person experiencing disharmony might have no idea this issue exists. For example, if someone were sensitive to perfume but didn't realize it, he or she might suddenly feel fatigued and might blame it on lack of sleep the night before, the need for food, or some other logical-sounding excuse. All of these could be valid, but it might also be the physical reaction to the perfume that entered the room.

Just recently, I had a meeting in my home, and during the discussion, one woman began to clear her throat and lightly cough. I hadn't noticed this behavior when she first arrived. The coughing and throat clearing continued to intensify. She apologized and said she didn't know why she was coughing. I asked her if she had any allergies. She answered that she was not aware of any. I was burning a candle that was fragrant. My little voice in my head told me to put it out. I put a lid on top of the candle to smother it out and stop the scent from continuing to permeate the room. I noticed that within a couple of minutes, she stopped coughing and was perfectly fine. She apparently had a sensitivity to something in the candle. It was not appropriate for me to test her at the time, so I am unable to be sure of what was going on. These scenarios happen daily to many people.

The problem with sensitivities is that most people are unaware of them. Without the awareness that the issue exists, nothing can be done to correct the disharmony. When it becomes a severe enough reaction that it disrupts life, most people will find an allergist or take medication or do something to alleviate the discomfort.

Oftentimes, when people with allergies have tests, the milder sensitivities don't even show up. When I test people using applied kinesiology, I find reactions to substances that were not previously revealed. I believe the energy system of the body is much more acute and refined than modern testing equipment. My experience with clients has convinced me of this.

In the following case, I asked Veronica about food allergies. She said according to her allergist, she was allergic to many things, but food was not among them. She had such a strong reaction to citrus that I found it hard to believe that her allergist hadn't diagnosed food allergies. Apparently, the tests that were done had not included citrus, or the reaction had not shown up in the results.

Veronica's Story in Her Own Words

I've had allergies since I can remember. I knew that eating fruit, especially fresh fruit, would irritate the back of my throat. I would use a metal fork to scratch my throat. When I was about twenty years old, I finally saw an allergy specialist. I had needles on my back that tested for different allergens. Depending on the size of swelling, they would determine how allergic I was to the item. They found I was allergic to weeds, trees, flowers, animals, and other things. But they didn't find any food allergies.

I had an orange tree in my yard, and I told my neighbor Hoberleigh that she could have some oranges because I was allergic and couldn't eat them. That was when she offered to clear my allergy. I was apprehensive about having a treatment with Hoberleigh. I didn't believe it would do anything, and I told my husband that she was a crazy lady who thought she could heal people. She kept asking me if she could help, so I finally decided to let her give it a go. I figured, *What the heck?*

We were in her treatment room, when she had me hold the orange in my hand, and she gave me the treatment. At first, I was skeptical. I was not feeling comfortable as she began. I was feeling tense, but as she continued with the treatment, I began to relax and was able to take comfortable, deep breaths. I remember while she was working on me, I experienced intense chills throughout my body, especially on my cheeks. My body felt ice cold. Then the sensations began to diminish. I had to hold the orange throughout the treatment. I remember she had me smell it. She asked me to return the next day to retest me. She said I was clear of the allergy. She wanted me to taste the orange to see if I had a reaction, but I still didn't believe anything had changed. I sliced open the orange, and I took a tiny taste and swallowed it. I waited for my throat to begin itching, but much to my surprise, it didn't. So I took a bigger bite. Still no reaction. Next thing I knew, I ate five whole oranges in a row. I have been eating oranges ever since.

On another occasion, I was making sweet-and-sour chicken or something using pineapple as an ingredient. I mentioned to Hoberleigh that I couldn't use fresh pineapple because it caused me to use a fork to scratch my throat. She persuaded me to see her again to release that allergy. During that treatment, she had me hold a bowl with fresh pineapple in it. I couldn't stand the smell of the pineapple. During the treatment, I had a similar reaction to the oranges. I felt the cold and chills throughout my body. I remember that Hoberleigh said I couldn't eat the pineapple for twenty-four hours. As she finished the treatment, the pineapple began to smell really good. I asked her if I could eat some, but she said no, that I had to wait. Much to our surprise, I dug in. Hoberleigh looked terrified and yelled, "Don't eat it yet!" We both waited to see what would happen, but there was no reaction. I was fine, and to this day, I eat pineapple. She has since treated me for animal allergies and roses and a few other things. I no longer call her "the crazy lady." Now highly I recommend her, and I am no longer a skeptic.

Hoberleigh's Version

I worked on Veronica soon after studying Nambudripad's Allergy Elimination Technique,* also known as NAET. That was back in the year 2000. In those days, we were taught a much more complex system of testing and treating allergies in a specific order. This was one of the few rules I chose not to follow, because it could take years to address the allergy that the client wanted addressed, not to mention all the extra money it would cost the person. All of that is against my principles. I did, however, follow the protocol of the individual session to the letter. That included having the client stay away from the allergen for twenty-four hours. I believed if the client ate, inhaled, touched, or otherwise contacted the allergen, he or she would still have the normal reaction. I also feared it would nullify the treatment. I was told it takes twenty-four hours for the energy to process through the twelve bilateral meridians. (These are the energetic pathways used in acupuncture. There are two other major meridians that travel through the midline of the body, but these were not addressed in this particular protocol.)

I learn a lot from giving treatments. One of the greatest things I learned from working on Veronica was that the person doesn't have to stay away from the allergen. When I saw her eat the pineapple, I wasn't sure if I should call 911, run across the street to get her inhaler, or hold her down so that she wouldn't stick a metal fork down her throat, as she threatened to do. To my great relief, she had no reaction whatsoever, but boy, was my heart pounding!

I learned that once the treatment is complete, everything that is released is permanently released—at least most of the time. I have had a few cases where there was still a reaction, but in each case, the reaction was less intense. Usually testing and clearing each of the acupuncture meridians is sufficient. This is because the meridians affect and influence each organ, gland, system, and part of the body directly or indirectly. Sometimes a specific organ, gland, or body part needs a specific treatment. When I test following the treatment and find the allergy has cleared, I assume it is done and there is no more to do. Most times, that is true. There are occasions when the body tests clear (with no reaction) following the treatment, yet the client returns complaining that there is still a reaction. It might be that the majority of the energetic frequency causing the reaction is gone but that the body needs time to process what has been released before it can let go of another part. It might be that I didn't form my question correctly when I tested. Or it might be that the allergy treatment was complete after all and that the current allergic reaction is due to something else entirely. I have encountered that situation on a number of occasions.

Patrice's Story

Patrice came to see me for allergies to animals. In those days, I used vials that held energy frequencies to test and clear allergies. I had her hold the vial for animals, and sure enough, she tested positive. She told me it was difficult for her to visit friends with pets because of her allergies. I cleared her for the energy of animals, and the next time I saw her, she let me know that animals no longer bothered her. However, when I saw her a few months later, she told me that she had visited her mother-in-law out of state and had had a strong reaction to her mother-in-law's cat, Angus. She told me the allergic reaction was usually so strong that she feared ending up in the emergency room. This time, it had been different. She'd had an obvious allergy attack, but at least she hadn't ended up at the hospital.

This puzzled and frustrated me. I don't like things to be incomplete. I retested her with the animal vial, and she showed no reaction. She confirmed that she had no reaction to any other animals. Not knowing anything about her relationship with her mother-in-law, I must admit that I assumed the worst. I thought maybe there was a problem between the two of them, and her body was physicalizing some emotional issue. I asked her about the relationship, but she said there were no problems. I thought there might be a chance she was not wanting to admit a problem, so I silently tested to see what her body said. To my surprise, her body agreed that she was telling the truth.

Then I tested the name Angus. She had a huge reaction. I went back and tested *cat*. No reaction. I then tested *Angus the cat*. Big reaction. On a conscious level, I don't recall her having any dislike or issue with the cat. This was the first time I had ever encountered someone having a reaction to one specific animal, so I wanted to delve in to get more information. I asked all kinds of questions. What came up startled me. I will freely admit that to this day, I have trouble believing the story that was revealed.

Here it goes. This was not the first lifetime in which Patrice and Angus the cat had met. There was a past life of them together. Angus had attacked and killed Patrice. We had to go in and clear out all past-life issues between the two of them.

Were they people? Were they animals? Were they both? I don't recall all the details, and to me, it doesn't really matter. I know many people will take issue with this information. I'm not here to tell anyone what the truth is about life, past lives, future lives, etc. All I do during a session is ask the questions and treat the issues that come up. What I know for sure is that once everything was released, Patrice no longer had a reaction to Angus when I tested.

The real test was what would happen when she was in contact with Angus. Back in those days, I used a machine that could duplicate a frequency of any substance and transfer that frequency into water. I made a little bottle of *Angus water* for Patrice just in case she had

a reaction. She informed me she would soon be going out of town to
visit her mother-in-law.

When she returned, she told me that she'd had a slight allergic
reaction to the cat—just a few sniffles. She had taken of few drops of
the Angus water, and the reaction had disappeared. She never had a
reaction to Angus after that.

Robert's Story

Robert is a handsome, athletic man who had suffered from a
bothersome allergy to ash trees for years.

One day, he was scheduled for a visit. When I opened the door
and looked out, however, I was shocked to see teary, swollen eyes in a
puffy, fevered red face. He was sniffling, sneezing, clearly miserable,
and hardly recognizable.

He explained that he was allergic to ash trees at this time of year,
when they bloomed. He had removed a large ash tree from his front
yard, but ash trees also grew everywhere in his neighborhood. When
they flowered, the result was the allergic reaction I was now seeing
in his unhappy face. Short of asking the entire neighborhood to cut
down all of their ash trees (something he deemed highly unlikely), he
didn't know what to do to solve this problem.

Robert had been to a number of allergists. Over the years, he had
received a bit of relief from prescription and over-the-counter drugs,
but these drugs frequently had undesirable side effects. When he
stopped the drugs, however, the symptoms from the allergy made
him feel miserable.

I had him hold the leaves and blooms from an ash tree in his
hand, and as I tested, I found that the difficulty was affecting almost
all of his meridians. (No wonder he had such an intense reaction!)

As I stroked his back to release the sensitivity, he said he could
feel a tingling sensation moving along his spine. I recall having to clear
not only each meridian but also the layers within each meridian.

Finally, after completing many levels of the treatment, Robert tested clear. As he was leaving, I noticed that his symptoms—the sniffing and watering eyes—were already diminishing. He telephoned later to tell me that the swelling in his face was almost gone and that he was feeling much better. Since that visit and treatment, Robert's allergic reaction to ash trees has not recurred.

Sometime later, after our success with the treatment for the allergy to ash trees, Robert told me that he also was allergic to roses. If he sat near roses for more than ten or fifteen minutes when they were in bloom, he would begin to sneeze and become congested, and his eyes would water.

This was a more complicated allergy, with both physical and emotional components. It took three sessions to clear Robert's sensitivity. The first two sessions involved treating him on the physical level. Even after these first sessions were complete, however, Robert still tested positive.

Looking deeper, we came upon an underlying emotional issue: an unconscious connection to his father, whom Robert positively and closely identified with. Robert reported that his father was allergic to roses, so on some deep level, Robert believed that he should be as well.

Once we uncovered this belief in our third session, we replaced it with the new belief that Robert did not have to be allergic to roses, as his father was, to still enjoy the positive connection they shared.

Since this time, Robert's positive connection to his father remains, but all traces of the allergy to roses are completely gone.

My Own Story

When I was around eleven or twelve years old, my mother decided to hunt for a larger home for our family. Because I loved to look at houses, she would sometimes take me with her. While we were looking at the house we eventually moved into, my mother asked me what I thought of it. I said to her, "It's okay, but if you buy this house, then I want the master bedroom." It was a huge room with three walk-in closets.

I have no idea why I had the audacity to even say those words to my mother or why she would have considered such a thing. My parents ended up buying the house, and to my shock, she decided to allow my older sister and me to share the master bedroom. I certainly couldn't complain. Half a master bedroom was better than none.

We moved in one week before school let out for the summer. That summer, I developed an annoying allergy. I don't know what I was allergic to, but it particularly bothered me at night. All night long, I would snort and sniffle and make honking noises. (Think of Felix Unger in the old *Odd Couple* sitcom.)

I don't know how my sister stood it as long as she did. In the middle of the next school term, she could take it no longer. She complained to my parents, and they allowed her to move into the tiny bedroom that our family had been using primarily for storage. Now I had the master bedroom to myself.

As mysteriously as the allergies had appeared, they disappeared. I didn't question it at the time, because I was so grateful for the relief. I had never taken any medication or had any treatments for the allergies. They were just gone. It wasn't until I was an adult that I thought more about it.

About ten or fifteen years after the incident, I was reading Louise Hay's book about the cause of certain conditions, when it occurred to me that my body (or, probably more accurately, my unconscious or subconscious mind) had figured out a way for me to have the master bedroom all to myself. My conscious mind was certainly not clever enough to do so. I just think it was a strange coincidence.

It's no secret (or maybe it is to some) that illness often has a benefit. It might get us the attention we desire. Or it might be something else. Our bodies have their own consciousness. An illness might be the body's way of serving us by providing an excuse we are seeking. Mind you, I don't mean to say we are intentionally trying to create an illness. It could be the effect of thoughts we are holding. That is why it's always a good idea to focus on what we want rather than on what we don't want.

Chapter 16

Trauma Relief

Probably my favorite thing to do is help people overcome the emotions of traumatic events that are still affecting them. The process can be much simpler than people think. What determines the ease of release is not how traumatic the event was or even how long ago it occurred. The determining factor seems to be the length of time in which the event took place. If the trauma was not a single episode but, rather, a recurring theme, such as being the recipient of abuse over years, then it takes longer to release. But if the event happened just once, then it's usually cleared in a single session.

I treated a man who wanted to be cleared from a traumatic experience he had as a child. When he was twelve years old, he went camping with his family in the mountains. His father asked him and his younger brother to gather sticks for the campfire. He gave them a compass and taught them how to use it so that they wouldn't get lost. As my client and his five-year-old brother scavenged for kindling, they came close to the edge of a cliff. When he yelled to his brother to move away from the edge, his brother became startled and dropped the compass he was holding. It went over the edge of the cliff. I could see much emotion overcome this man as he continued with his story.

"I got very angry with my brother, and I told him he was going to get into big trouble for losing the compass," he explained. He continued to make his way back to camp. He heard a noise, and when he turned back around to see what the cause was, his brother was gone. His brother must have tried to retrieve the compass but then had fallen off the cliff. This man had been living with incredible guilt at being the cause of his younger brother's death.

I tested him to find the acupuncture meridians where the energy of the memory was locked in. It only took about twenty minutes to clear him from the trauma of this event. Once he tested clear, I asked him how he felt. He said he felt as if a thousand pounds had been lifted from his body. I asked him to recount the story, and I watched him closely for an emotional response. His face remained calm as he retold the story. When it was complete, I questioned him again as to how he felt.

He admitted that it was a sad thing that had happened, but he no longer felt the overpowering guilt. He knew it had been an accident, and he believed that his brother would forgive him. More importantly, he could finally forgive himself.

I am pleased to include testimonials from a couple of my clients in their own words.

> I have suffered from post-traumatic stress for as long as I can remember. I didn't know what it was when I was young, only that life was scary and unpredictable.
>
> In 2000, my mother was diagnosed with lung cancer. I spent as much time with her as I could, and after eight months, she died. This was, of course, traumatic, and I thought I was dealing with it better than I could have expected. Turns out that I was in shock. This left me almost paralyzed, as each day I sat on the sofa, becoming more and more agoraphobic. I knew I had to do something when I could not even go outside to get the mail.

So I managed to make it to the doctor's office, where they happily prescribed antidepressants for me. The first one I tried worked! It worked so well that I was euphoric. Happier than I had been all my life. I was also able to read much better. Retaining information rather than having to reread everything made it possible to read a few books a day. My brain was taking in all the information going on around me and understanding it.

Needless to say, I was far from being depressed. If this was what drugs could do for me, then I was willing to be a drug addict. After all, for the first time in my life, I wasn't afraid or anxious.

I could not have imagined what happened next. I woke up one day, and the old me was there! I knew it as soon as I stood up. The awful feeling in my gut and in my head was there, only it felt much stronger than I remembered. Because it was!

Somehow the antidepressant medication reversed, and I was sliding down a slippery slope faster than I could get a handle on what was going on. I got to the doctor somehow, where, you guessed it, they put me on more drugs.

I never was able to recover what I felt like after the first round of meds and actually got more and more unstable until I knew I would have to get off the four antidepressants they had me taking at that point. I went to the doctor and asked how I should go about it and was told to go off of them gradually, which I did.

I came back to my old self more anxious and suffering from what they call ADD. This was a devastating condition that took up most of my day looking for things I couldn't find, missing appointments, and losing track of time.

The most damaging aspect of it for me was the frustration I would experience and the tantrums and fits of rage. This always left me more devastated than anything because of the embarrassment of it, as I would often yell and scream and throw stuff, adding to the mess of things already piling up around me in the confusion and inability to organize my life.

I started going to the Church of Truth, where I met Hoberleigh. We connected right away. I felt comfortable around her due to her nonjudgmental attitude. I had seen her work with others and could feel the sincerity of her work. It seemed so simple, and I wasn't sure if it could do anything for me. One day, she just offered, and I said yes.

I felt different right away. When I spoke of a couple of traumatic events after her treatments, they didn't have the same gut-wrenching feeling as before. After a week passed, I had dropped the frustration level to almost nothing. I am very grateful. I still experience some ADD symptoms, though they are getting less and less with each passing day. Without the frustration, ADD does not dominate my life any longer. I can actually have a life.

I kept waiting for the effects to wear off, as they did with my first round of antidepressants. They haven't. It is still working, and it is doing so a little bit more each day.

It does seem like magic. That's because it is. For anyone who thinks magic isn't real, I can tell them that it most certainly is real.

My respect and gratitude are overflowing. Thank you, my friend Hoberleigh.

Jacqueline Grace

And the following is from another client:

In 1979, after many kinds of treatment, my forty-two-year-old sister died of ovarian cancer. In 2001, a second sister died from this disease. After therapy and much grief counseling did not lessen the grief, I found Hoberleigh, and she was able to help me with my grief. I now can think of my sisters and recall the love, the joy, and the fun, not the sorrow and loss. But I did not realize the power the disease still held over me outside of grief emotions.

Recently, a dear friend was undergoing surgery for ovarian cancer, and I found myself unable to pray for her or even send words of love. I was overwhelmed with anger, hopelessness, and fear.

The first thought I had for help was Hoberleigh. I contacted her, and she did her tests for beliefs the body is holding. She had me place my fingertips on my wrist and forehead, and she gently stroked my back. At first, chills spread throughout my body, but after a few minutes, I felt a shift, and the chills left me.

Driving home from the treatment, I said, "Ovarian cancer," out loud to myself, and I was overjoyed that the first thought that came to my mind was *Many people survive this disease, and many new therapies are now available.* And I believed it!

I am now able to pray for my friend with prayer that is not struggling through anger and fear. I was able to see my friend and freely rejoice in her rapid recovery from the surgery. Hoberleigh's help freed my soul from emotions that were keeping me prisoner, and I am most grateful. I know that, like the grief healing, this is a permanent fix!

Maryann Wesson

I had been facilitating a weekly class where I would periodically ask participants if they had an issue they would like to have tested, and possibly treated, during the class. The following is the story of one young woman who volunteered during one of these sessions. She included some interesting history regarding her issue which I have edited out. You will find her complete story on my blog.

"Not again! Really?" Here I am, lying in my bed, starring at the mono-chromatic white ceiling, with my life force pretty much evaporated. I can barely move due to my lack of getting air into my lungs, and going to the bathroom is an expedition that needs to be carefully rationed and planned out. Every year it's the same story. The same thing happens at the same time. Unbelievable! Or is it? Just like clockwork, ever since I can remember, my body and the rest of me, are out of commission for two whole weeks out of the year. It is hard to remember the exact onset of this thing since I have had to live with it more years than not. No matter where I was, no matter what I was doing or not doing, about two weeks before my birthday in March, I would get faint cold-like symptoms. Every year I act surprised and wonder whether my symptoms relate to spring time allergies or are merely a part of a residual cold epidemic that somehow escaped me in the winter.

"Today we are going to work on releasing physical problems. Does anybody have anything for me to work on and perhaps release?" Pause—pause, blink-blink . . . *Oh, do I have something for you to work on, I smugly thought to myself.* Although I had heard about advanced energy work, and did believe it to be an alternative healing modality, I felt that my situation was a little too challenging perhaps. My heart was pounding fast, and even though I questioned the efficacy of this energy work, something inside of me believed that perhaps, I could be able to get some relief from this curse after all, for a small exchange of exposing my chronic health issue to the group. *How bad can this be? I thought to myself . . . After all, I am at MY church, with MY people, and in a safe environment. I know this healer and respect her work profoundly . . . So, why not? Well, if she decides to pick me, that is.*

"Ok, I have something for you, Hoberleigh." And so, I began informing her and the group of the invisible monster that had plagued me throughout my whole entire life. As predicted, murmurs and widely opened eyes engulfed my body, and despite cherishing the sincerity of this present group, I could not help but wonder if I was a freak. Was I? Come to think of it, who is not?

Not really assuming she would pick me out of the crowd, Hoberleigh did. "I will muscle test you. Stretch out your right hand and strengthen it. Don't let me push it down. Resist my force."

Sure, I thought. *Let's see what happens. This should be interesting.*

Within a few seconds, Hoberleigh broke the silence by verbalizing her amazement: "Oh wow! Wait a minute. Can this be?" *Care to clarify? I thought to myself. Can what be?* I voiced my concerns. "Wait a minute." *Ok, this is too much! Every time I go to the doctor's office or something like that, I always get the same response.* "This is interesting." *or* "I have never seen that before." Though I now have confirmed that I'm *not* a freak, these comments do not help in that department. To prove my point even further, you know how on every medical prescription there is this warning label stating that 1% of the time patients might experience X, Y, and Z side-effects? Well, there was a time my friend would call me *side-effects* girl because I am that 1%. It's kind of morbidly fascinating how that works.

"I have only seen one other case like this." Hoberleigh confirmed. *Oh, so now I am a case?* As a mental health therapist I am very familiar with this terminology. But this was different. We were dealing with unseen stuff here. But before I could even voice my objection to the word *case,* Hoberleigh lovingly and sympathetically proceeded. "So, blockages can be held in different parts of you, such as in your body, your subconscious mind, etc . . . Yours however, seems to be in the soul."

In my soul? Did I hear correctly? That is just wonderful! Never mind I have issues, but my soul has them too? That is just fantastic! Not only am I shocked about this reality, but those large, wide opened eyes were still looking at me. I know what you must be thinking. I was thinking the same.

"Okay, no problem," Hoberleigh reassured me she knew what she was doing. "Turn around, I am going to clear you." Pause—pause, blink—blink. "How do you feel?" *How do I feel? Really?* "Ahh, I feel the same." I replied, refusing to believe that a quick clearing would salvage my soul.

"Let me muscle test you again," Hoberleigh said. Pause-pause, blink-blink. "Ok, how about now?" *Come on*, I thought to myself. "Ahh, still feeling the same. Wait, what exactly am I supposed to be feeling here?" I asked her with great wonder.

"Can you stay after class? I would like to work on you some more" Hoberleigh reached out her verbal hand toward me. The last few minutes of this spiritually minded Thursday night class is a blur to me as I was still trying to figure out what just happened and what was about to happen in the near future.

After class, Hoberleigh pulled me aside. Though unofficially invited, some of my peers lingered around, hoping to witness something. Innocently she asked me "So, remind me, when do you typically get sick? Isn't it between your birthday in March and Valentine's day?"

"Yeah" I answer with my head hanging in a discouraged position. "Hmmmm, that is interesting." *See! See what I mean. There goes that comment! It never fails! Even a spiritual holistic healer views my case as interesting. Inconceivable!*

"Well, let's think about this," Hoberleigh proceeded as she interrupted my gaze into nowhere and everywhere. "Naturally, your birthday marks the day you were born. And Valentine's day is . . . wait a minute? "Did you ever have a traumatic break up or something by any chance?" I reminded her that this stuff began at age 5? "Oh yes, that is right. Well, either way, I think there is an issue regarding love or self—love maybe?" *Self-love? Come on. Don't give me that!* Sure, my self-esteem could use a boost once in a while, but that was not it. I could feel it.

Then, all of a sudden, I was reminded of something I had tried to stuff away since the beginning of time. *If she is really that good, she will figure this out on her own, I thought to myself in a testy way.* And before I would finish enjoying the parameters I had set for myself, Hoberleigh's loving eyes connected with mine, and in a whispering tone of disbelief asked me "Do you have a hard time being here . . . on this earth?"

Streams of tears rolled down my face as if the flood gates of my soul had opened. *Hard time? That is an understatement! Yes I have a hard time! I always have.* Ever since I can remember, my mom had explained to me that I have "Muehe am Leben." This from the German translated would mean "having a difficult time living." Mom knew or felt it all along How sad this reality of mine must have been for her. I can only imagine.

Allow me to explain and interject something here. Having "Muehe am Leben" has nothing to do with feeling suicidal and everything to do with just feeling tired of living, even since age 5.

"Is that it?" Hoberleigh was looking for a confirmation. Although my intent was to verbally communicate with her, I could not. My throat felt like it was closing and I felt I had entered a tornado zone where everything became unbalanced. As my tears multiplied, so did my breath, and I was trying desperately to take control of my inhalations or my exhalations, which ever would prove to be easier.

"OK, take a deep breath and tell yourself that you forgive yourself for being born." Oh man, those were the magical *no-can-do* words. How can I forgive myself if I don't want to forgive myself? Ponder that one. Within a split second, this tornado feeling that I had been experiencing just underwent some kind of centrifugal process because my internal winds were now blowing in each and every direction. I was now crying and sobbing out of control. My body was even shaking. I immediately knew I was at an impasse. I knew I had to somehow muster enough courage and strength to cross this threshold. There was no turning back. I could feel it.

"How about saying 'I am at peace being here? Can you say that?" *Well, I figured that the word "peace" might be a little easier to roll out of my mouth than the word "forgive," plus, if I say it many times, as was suggested, perhaps I will believe and internalize this concept at some point. I will try this, but I am not feeling this.*

Witnessing my increasing discomfort, Hoberleigh began to stroke my back in an attempt to calm me down. "I am going to start clearing your back, and clear these feelings forever, from this life time to many other future life times. You might feel a little nauseous or might even feel as if you might be experiencing flu symptoms. Ready?" I gathered all my remaining energy together to give her a halfhearted noncommitting nod. "Feel anything?" "Nope! I am good," I replied, slightly rolling my eyes internally. "How about now?" "Nope, I am . . . oh my God! My whole body is shaking, and I feel like I am about to throw up! I feel like I have the chills and I am dizzy! Oh God! I am so dizzy!"

"Good! This is very good! I am going to keep clearing you." *Good? How the hell is this good? I feel like I am about to faint here!* Reading my mind perhaps, she told me to "just trust the process. Trust me, this is good!" Hoberleigh reassured me. Then, she told me to repeat some words after her. Whereas some words were to help with the clearing process, others were intended for the *reconstruction of beliefs* phase, I concluded. Unfortunately, I can't write about this experience because even in the moment, I was having a difficult time remembering what I needed to repeat since I felt I was somewhere far, far away.

My initial concerns of looking like a fool or a freak quickly subsided. I did not even remember the wide opened eyes from my peers who were pretending not to look. I did not have time for trivialities. I was in the middle of having my soul worked on. No wonder none of the more traditional therapies never worked with addressing my noble issue of "Muehe am Leben" syndrome. Though I could not exactly remember what Hoberleigh had said or what I was supposed to reiterate and repeat, I make up for in remembering how my body felt. I felt not here nor there, and with every clearing she blessed me with, my body was reacting to this process like an accordion. Although I felt many different kinds of emotions, happiness and joy were not among the many. I felt as if my body was a towel that was being wrung out and twisted by the universe. I felt currents of something bolting through my body. I felt like I was a puppet, being pulled and stretched by the strings of the puppeteer. I felt that if this experiment was going to go south, something very bad would stick with me, for this state I was in was one to be visited, not lived in.

How long this clearing took, I will never know. It was definitely more than five minutes and perhaps less than ten. Time has always been a relative concept to me, so why would it be any different when I am being rebooted? Just like after an earthquake when all the rumbling and shaking suddenly comes to a halt, so this too abruptly came to a finale. But instead of needing to pick up all the pieces from the collateral damage the natural disaster would have left behind, my natural, internal disaster seemed to have vanished. There I stood in the middle of the room, not quite sure what had hit me and not quite sure how my life was going to unravel from here on.

As soon as Hoberleigh had stopped clearing me, all my crazy feelings and physical discomforts vanished like a raccoon at sunrise. *Hmmmm, so, might this be it? Can ten minutes really cancel out a life time of bed ridden, life depleting, I-am-a-fish-out-of-the-water feeling and gift me my life back? I guess time will tell.* It so happened that my birthday would be in a few months. *The proof will be in the pudding, I thought.*

I thanked my friend and gave her a love donation, an uncertain amount that would serve as an energetic exchange for her work. How much do you give a person who might have lifted a life-long curse?

Fast forward to three years later

I am humbled and blessed to announce that since my healing encounter with Hoberleigh, I have not gotten sick once! Birthdays have come and gone and . . . nothing, no need for an extended bed rest. In addition, I am humbled as well as perplexed to be a solid believer that our bodies and our minds are not the only ones that can have issues. Our souls can as well. No wonder traditional therapies are sometimes limited to taking the scenic route to healing and recovery. After reading this story, you might still be baffled as to why, exactly, my soul experienced issues to begin with. Although I do not have all of the answers that adorn this mystery, I do have a good working hypothesis. Suffice to say that not all realities can be seen with the naked eye or even understood with traditional logic or reason. Some things are just between you and God.

Chapter 17

Things You Can Do

Talk to Your Body

I believe every organ, gland, cell, and part of the body has its own consciousness. I believe the body receives our thoughts and words without judgment. Though it has consciousness, it doesn't have volition to make the choices. The body follows our words and thoughts, which can be considered commands. Here are a couple of stories illustrating why I believe this is the case.

Years ago, I read a book written by a medical intuitive. She walked into an operating room to observe a surgery. She had permission to observe, but she was late in arriving, and the operation was already in progress. As she entered, she heard screaming. She looked around to see who was in so much distress. The room was filled with voices, which were saying things like "What's going on?" and "No one told me what was happening!" and "What are you doing with me?"

She noticed all of the doctors and nurses were carrying on as though they heard nothing. She then realized the voices were coming from the organs and body parts being affected by the surgery. Because of her incredible heightened sense of awareness, she was the only one who could hear the organs screaming. She ran out of the room, overwhelmed by the experience.

It was then that she realized that body parts have consciousness. She began a new practice of working with patients who were scheduled to undergo surgery. Using her newly acquired information, she would schedule appointments with patients to communicate with the body to let it know what to expect during surgery. She would also be in the operating room during the surgery, explaining procedures as they occurred. Finally, she would follow up after the surgery, once again talking with the body parts. None of the patients she worked with experienced any complications during or following the surgeries.

After reading this story, I found out the daughter of a friend of mine was scheduled for surgery. I asked him if she was open to weird stuff that might help her make it a better experience. He didn't know but said he would relay any information I gave him to let her decide what to do with it. I summarized what I had read, and he thought it was interesting and worth considering.

He gave his daughter the information, and she was open to giving it a try. I understand her surgery went beautifully. She came through it with flying colors. Not only that, but she needed almost no pain medication following the surgery and recovered much more quickly than the doctor had seen before. He told her that whatever she was doing, she should continue with it.

Another friend was scheduled for cervical vertebrae fusion. After I related the story of the medical intuitive's tale, he asked his daughter to talk to his organs before the surgery and then later in the recovery room.

This is what he told me: "I did a number of affirmations before my surgery and had a written list of things that I asked the anesthesiologist to say during the surgery, such as telling me while I was under anesthesia that the operation was going well, everything was fine, I would wake up and heal quickly, etc. The anesthesiologist said he did this. I had that paper [with the affirmations] in my room with me as well. My surgery went very well, and so did my recovery."

In fact, his daughter shared with me that his recovery took less than half the time they had thought it would for a man his age.

There is another story I read that has helped to convince me of the consciousness of our body parts. This was about a journalist (I'll call him Mike) who was interviewing a medical intuitive. After the interview, she evaluated the journalist's body and found that Mike's spleen was confused. According to his spleen, it was following what it thought Mike wanted it to do, but apparently this was causing some problems. Mike gave the spleen new instructions with much love and care, and the spleen began to change how it was functioning in order to follow the new directions. Soon after, the spleen said it felt a lot of anger directed at it and became confused. It didn't know what it had done wrong.

When the intuitive gave Mike the news, he gave his side of the story. Mike had gone to the doctor and had been diagnosed with some condition involving the spleen. Because he knew about talking to his body, he began to do so. After a time, he went back to the doctor but did not get the good news he had been expecting. He was disappointed that his condition wasn't healing fast enough. He became impatient and angry with his spleen.

All of this sounds illogical, I admit. I have found when I follow the logical mind and ignore the information that comes from left field, I regret it. Since I have started listening to my body and my little voices, I find that life works much more smoothly and effortlessly.

Here is my own story regarding communicating with my body. During a genome healing class, we were instructed to ask a body part some questions. My eyesight is not what I would like it to be, and I have been working on correcting my vision for some time. About twenty-seven years ago, I had radial keratotomy surgery to correct my vision. This was before the laser procedure that is done today. A surgeon made eight cuts in each eye with a scalpel to flatten the cornea. It was extremely painful later that day when the topical anesthesia wore off, but the results were well worth the pain. I had perfect vision for about twenty years. Then my vision began to blur, and I have since learned that is often the case with this particular surgery.

During the class, I chose to talk to my eyes. I asked them what was going on and how they were feeling. I was unexpectedly overwhelmed with sadness. Tears fell due to the deep emotional pain I was feeling, and from within, a voice said, *They cut us! We didn't do anything wrong! We don't understand why we were cut. It wasn't our fault. Why did they have to cut us?*

I used a process we were taught in the class to help organs in distress, and after using the technique, within just a couple of minutes, the sadness dissipated. I was truly shocked by what I had just experienced. I'd had no idea this sadness even existed. The surgery had been so long ago that I never would have believed the pain would still be there. I admit my vision has not improved since that time, so outwardly, nothing changed, but on some level, something happened. It was a profound experience for me. I definitely felt a shift within my being

The message here is to consider communicating with your body in beneficial ways. It can't hurt—at least not when you do it in private. No one needs to know. This is strictly between you and your body.

So many of us already communicate with and to our bodies without forethought. Have you ever said, "This breaks my heart"? What if your heart hears you and thinks you are giving instructions? Can you absolutely say for sure this is not occurring? Would you bet your life on it? You just might be doing so without realizing it. What about "This is a pain in the neck," or "This gives me a headache," or even "I'd give my right arm for that"? Words are powerful, and few people recognize the energy in our words. Even those of us who are aware frequently have lapses and tend to create unintentional manifestations through misuse of language.

I ask my friends to keep me on track when they hear me speaking in a negative manner. We don't hear it in ourselves nearly as well as we hear it in another person. In any case, learn to love and appreciate your body, both as a whole and as individual parts. The more love and gratitude you send it, the more potential you have for better health.

The Power of Visualizing

I probably have enough stories on this topic to write another book, but I will only share one story here. More than a decade ago, I was part of a prosperity group. There were six of us, and we met once a week. One of the agreements we made to each other was to pray (however we chose) for prosperity for each member of the group on a daily basis.

I was invited by a friend to attend a Sunday service at the Self-Realization Fellowship Lake Shrine Temple in Pacific Palisades. Sometime during the service, I chose to pray for my prosperity group. I began to visualize each group member, including myself, sitting in a circle. In my mind's eye, I saw money falling from above, showering down within and around our little group.

Visualization, as I've studied, means more than just seeing something happen. It means including all the sensations of an experience, involving as many of the five senses as one is able. I not only saw the money fall but also felt the paper money brushing softly against my skin and smelled the scent of money around me. (Money does have a certain scent to it, especially new bills.)

Perhaps only a few minutes passed. I remember the feeling of exhilaration while doing this. At the end of the service, the collection containers were passed along the rows. People were dropping in their tithes and offerings and passing the baskets to the person next to them. I was sitting on the end of the row on the right, waiting for the basket, which was being passed from the left. My friend was on my left, with a man sitting to her left. As he passed the basket to her, it hit her elbow and flew into the air, showering all of the money directly on me. It was all I could do to keep from laughing out loud.

I've told that story to a few people who said, "But you didn't get to keep the money," and I tell them I forgot to put that part in the visualization. No. I didn't get to keep the money. It's important to be specific and remember the details.

A few months later, I was talking with a gentleman who is a psychic. I related this story to him, and I asked him why that visualization had manifested so quickly. He closed his eyes and went into his state of meditation where he receives information. Then he responded, "Two reasons. First, the energy in that temple is of a very high vibration. And second, you visualized that scene with great joy. Joy is the emotion that manifests faster than any other emotion."

Since that time, I've thought about it, and I believe there was one other factor he didn't mention. Because I didn't really believe this vision was how we were going to manifest our money, I didn't have any limiting thoughts regarding that situation. Here are a few examples of limited thinking:

"Wow, how will this ever happen?"

"This will be really difficult."

"Do I deserve this?"

"What will other people say if I accomplish my goal?"

So many thoughts cross our minds that keep us from creating what we say we want. Had I done that, then the experience probably wouldn't have happened. Like I said, none of those thoughts entered my mind at all. I just played with the scenario for fun.

Two individuals who have written about visualization are Shakti Gawain and Neville. I learned a tremendous amount from the writings of both of these individuals. I would highly recommend the book *Creative Visualization* by Shakti Gawain.

The other author, Neville Goddard (best known as Neville), has written many books that inspire me. He is no longer here in body, but his works live on. I call his technique Nevillizing. In his book *Feeling Is the Secret*, he said, "You never attract that which you want but you always attract that which you are conscious of being. Prayer is the art of assuming the feeling of being and having that which you want."

In my little visualization with the falling money, I was having the experience in my mind. I wasn't wanting it to happen. I felt the experience of it. It might sound like a subtle detail, but I believe that is what makes the difference of manifesting something into this

3-D experience or not having it. I highly recommend looking up the website www.nevillegoddard.wwwhubs.com for more information. On his website, you will be able to read some of his works.

Tapping Away Pain

Half a dozen years ago, I was practicing yoga on a daily basis. Every day, I felt a stabbing pain in my ribs when I bent forward. The first few days, it was a slight discomfort that I ignored. As the days progressed, the pain increased. I was losing weight, which was a good thing that I needed to do, but as the weight decreased, the pain increased.

Eventually, the pain occurred at other times of the day, even when I wasn't doing yoga. I couldn't even bend over to tie my shoes without major cramping in the ribs. Finally, I couldn't stand it anymore. After not completing a yoga session because of the pain, I went home and sat in meditation. I asked for the cause of the pain. *Ask* might be a little too tame of a word. I *demanded* an answer.

My little voice spoke up in answer and replied, "This is the pain you had when you starved to death. Your ribs broke and punctured your lung."

Really? Once again, when something comes up that makes no sense, I have to pay attention because I know my logical mind had nothing to do with that answer. I decided to use the tapping method from the Emotional Freedom Techniques* protocol.

I used the setup phrase "Even though I have this pain from when I starved to death in a past life, I love and accept myself." Continuing with the protocol, I tapped on phrases like "this pain in my ribs," "starving to death in a past life," "broken ribs puncturing my lungs," and other similar phrases. I used this method just the one time for this particular issue. The process took about ten to fifteen minutes.

Not knowing whether anything had happened or not, I continued with my day. The next morning, as I began my yoga practice, I noticed the change. Without a doubt, I could tell the pain was gone. From that time on, I might have had a slight twinge now and then, but it was nothing like what I had experienced in the past. This was a major healing for me.

I find this method of tapping to be extremely useful when emotions come up that can't be contained. This was my first time having a successful outcome with a physical problem. But then again, I wasn't tapping on the pain itself but on the underlying cause that might or might not have been real.

Cord Cutting

I mentioned earlier that when I first began practicing energetic work, I ended up with symptoms similar to those of the individuals I had been working on. I have since learned that the energy or frequency of a disease or disharmony is no respecter of persons. When my energetic field was affected, I experienced the problem. Perhaps it was due to the fact that I was playing in their energetic field and it glommed on to me during the process.

I have learned ways to protect myself, and I will share a couple of tidbits here. First is the idea of cutting cords. I don't feel that I am the best person to explain this, as I hardly understand it myself. I am most grateful for permission to reproduce this information here.

The following article was written by Barbara McKell, Intuitive Healer, Reiki Master, and teacher. It is based on her personal experience and the methods she has found to be effective and lasting.

> Etheric cords can form between people, objects, and situations where there is a fearful attachment, afraid to let go, scared to be alone, afraid to be without. These are invisible energy links. We normally cord to other people

and also allow them to cord to us throughout the course of our everyday lives. Many of these cords are short lived and dissolve quickly. There are some however, normally the intensive, volatile, or the longer term relationships, that create cords and with a build-up of numerous energies and emotions, such as need, desire, love, anger, jealousy, envy, etc. These cords can create problems in the form of aches and pains, depression, rage, exhaustion, burn-out, etc.

Most people aren't even aware of these energy cords. The few that are aware can only vaguely describe their experiences, and the smallest handful of people who actually have high sensitivity are reluctant to speak about it. There are also a multitude of frauds, phonies, gurus and religious zealots who use cording to attach to their followers to make money.

It is normal for parents to form cords with their babies. This is both a necessity and a positive thing, as these cords help parents communicate with and understand their baby's needs. Healthy cords dissolve naturally over a period of time, as the child grows. Negative cords feed the energy and emotions of one person to another, both positive and negative, so you may be feeling particularly angry and not know why. You may also be feeling depressed for no apparent reason. Cords are normally formed on a subconscious level, through a person's need for strength, manipulation or control.

If you have decided to move on from a relationship and you find it particularly difficult to "let-go" it may be that there are cords of attachment from the other person holding you back. A person going through a divorce may be feeding their anger, rage, stress, and jealousy to the other person and vice versa. Without realizing it, parents feed these emotions to their children and partners, creating all sorts of problems for everyone.

If you have a cord attached to someone you love and that person is going through a major crisis, they may be draining energy from you. So you will feel drained without knowing why. In this case some healthy boundaries need to be created.

Can you cut them? I've discovered that just randomly cutting cords causes more harm than good. Any healing process requires a conscious awareness and respect for the fact that it is a process. It is better to work with the cords, and learn how to adapt and understand them. I believe we have choice about becoming attached by unhealthy cords if we are operating on an entirely conscious level. The first step you may need to take is to take a break from being around a person, given the intensity of the energy that flows between you. Sometimes these cords reach across time and space, so we have to work with them on all levels.

When we give power away to other people because our relationship with self is dysfunctional, we actually allow cords of energy to tie us to those people. You can cut the cords, but unless you resolve the underlying reason why you corded in the first place, the cords will keep coming back.

The following methods of cord removal I teach preclude removing any healthy cords and offer opportunity to heal the underlying issues.

Releasing the Cords

+ One method for removing the energy cords is to imagine yourself sitting on a big green lawn in a circle. The circle can be made of fine silken rope—literally a "cord". Sit in it, feel yourself protected by it. Imagine a column of light coming from the heavens encircling you in high frequency pure light.
+ Then imagine the people you want out of your life also sitting in a circle made of cord. The two circles are close to each other but not touching. Look at the other people from your circle and wave good

bye! You are gently and peacefully allowing other people their space while affirming your own. Instead of cutting, you are transmuting the cords. Let their cords remain whole. Let yours remain whole. Just disentangle and detach. Stoke the fires of love and compassion. Say good bye with love and move on!

As life is lived, the process of sorting and disentangling is obviously much more complex and subtle. As you make the music of your life less dysfunctional, the people attracted to the dysfunctional part will fall off. Chords are better than cords.

Higher-Self Work to Remove and Heal Cord Attachments

Connection to high self . . .

First do a mediation to align the client (or yourself if doing the work on yourself) with their high self.

Bring in the high self of the person with whom you have an unhealthy attachment.

Have the client (or yourself, if doing the work on yourself) imagine and call in the presence of the high self of the person with whom they feel they have unhealthy cords connected to. Remind them that this is the person's high self without all their fears, doubts and control issues. Have them imagine the person as their whole, light filled loving self. If they have difficulty just tell them to imagine it.

Speaking from the heart . . .

Once they feel the presence of the person, have them begin to tell the person how they feel about the past. Tell them to speak from their heart, telling the person about how they have hurt them and how they have suffered because of their relationship. They can do this silently if they are not comfortable speaking it out loud. Encourage them to get everything off their chest. And then once that is completed have them tell the person what it is that they need from them now.

Listening . . .

Now it is time for the high self of the other person to speak. Remind them that they are safe. This is the person's loving, true self, without fear or anger. Tell them that they are speaking from their heart now and telling them all the things they have needed to say. Ask them to listen now with an open heart and be willing to receive what they are being told. (It may be telepathic or come in as a feeling.) Encourage them to receive the information however it comes in. Have them ask the person what they need now.

Remind them that if they asked for forgiveness that forgiveness is not condoning but is making the decision not to carry it any longer.

Are you willing?

Now ask your client (or yourself if doing the work on yourself) if they are willing and ready to help this person with what it is that they need. It is okay if they are not willing to do anything for the other person. Ask them what they are willing to do for themselves.

Pruning the Garden.

Once this process feels complete I ask the client to call in a high spiritual being to assist them.

Tell them to look at the space between you and this person. There you will see attachments. Some will be healthy and light filled, some will be unhealthy looking, like the old dead branches on bushes and trees. Now ask your spirit guide to give you a tool to prune away all the dead and unhealthy looking connections. As you trim away these attachments your guide heals the places where they were cut away with healing light. You may help them select the perfect color of light to do this work with. Continue cutting away the unhealthy attachments until only the healthy light filled connections remain. Your guide will take the old cords and offer them to Mother Earth to be transmuted into new life. If the person you are doing this work with wants to help you . . . allow them to be part of the process. Once the pruning is complete and all the old connecting points are sealed with light. You now are free to end this relationship or continue it on a basis that is healthy for both of you. Thank the high self of the person you are working with and say good bye allowing them to return to whatever they were doing. Thank your high self and your guide and come back into waking consciousness.

Removing a cord is a three step process:

1. unplugging the cord
2. disposing of the cord
3. cleansing and healing the anchor point / attachment point.

Cord Pulling/Cutting

Some practitioners advocate cutting or removing all cords. Some attachments simply should not be removed because they are as yet too deeply engaged with our energy systems. Additionally, cord cutting can result in shocking both your energy system and that of the person on the other end, creating a host of unwanted sensations, feelings, and emotions. Cord pulling is safer, more effective, measurably gentler, and longer lasting. Cord pulling does not shock the system of either party, and allows the practitioner to more effectively heal and seal the connection points.

Although similar to cord cutting, cord pulling requires coming from a very compassionate perspective from both practitioner and client. It requires practice, using tempered skill adequately, repeatedly and with continued success.

In cord work, there is more than the practitioner and the client involved—there are others at the opposite end of each cord and they too must be taken cared of.

Pulling cords doesn't necessarily lead to break-ups or abandoned relationships, unless that is what you are seeking. Cord pulling will help you move forward with confidence and clarity since it releases the dysfunctional parts of your relationships. Fear is the opposite of love, and all attachments are created from fear.

If there are negative energy cords attached ask how many. If the number is large, begin with the most prominent. Begin pulling the cords one at a time. Handle them lovingly and then connect them to the positive energy of crystalline Earth grid. Repeat the process and continue pulling cords one by one and connect them immediately to the positive energy of crystalline Earth grid or dispose of them by placing them into a violet flame.

This information above comes from Barbara McKell, an Intuitive Healer in Guelph, Ontario, and can be found at www.soulconnection.ca.

When I work on an individual, I have my own protocol with my own little spin that I use based on the ThetaHealing classes I've taken. I sit with my eyes closed and imagine a white light coming from above me and pouring down through and around my body, washing everything in and around me into the ground. I wave my hand quickly and sharply down the front of my body to cut any cords that might have been established during a treatment with a client. I mentally disengage the roots of the cords from my body. I bless the cut ends that are still connected to the other person to free them from my energy. Then I imagine energy from my body moving from my tailbone down my legs, through the soles of my feet, through the floor, and deep into the earth to ground my energy. Finally, I bring that energy, which is now purified by the earth, back into my body through the soles of my feet, up my legs, and into my heart.

Protecting Yourself

This next tidbit is something I learned when studying Pranic Healing* with Master Stephen Co. When you walk into a room with a lot of tension, do you get an uncomfortable feeling? Are there times when you are around someone and you can sense an uncomfortable or negative energy? If you are able to do so and you want to protect yourself from being affected by that energy, then this information is for you.

Tuck your thumbs inside your fists and cross your arms over your solar plexus. (This is the soft spot just below the bottom of the breastbone.) Shift your body so that you are slightly turned with your right side to the individual giving off the negative vibes rather than facing him or her straight on. This helps to keep the solar-plexus chakra (the emotional chakra) from absorbing the negative energy. The chakras take in and expel energy constantly. You don't have to be obvious about the movement. This is an intuitive movement many people do automatically without conscious awareness.

Here's another tip. If you are in a class or a situation where you want to take in the information or the energy around you, then be sure to keep your arms uncrossed. You will be much more receptive.

Affirmative Prayer
Similar to Visualization

While studying the Science of Mind, I learned that there are five steps to this process.

Recognition: We recognize there is one Universal Source, or God—one infinite power that is omniscient, omnipresent, and omnipotent.

Unification: We are part of this Source. Because we are made in the image and likeness of God, we are co-creators and have the ability to co-create in our own lives.

Realization: We realize that what we choose to create already exists, though it is not yet manifested on the physical plane. Through contemplation, we are able to call it forth into our lives.

Thanksgiving: Once the first three steps have been correctly applied, we will be in a confident state of knowing our prayer is in motion, and we can give thanks that it is so.

Release: We let go and let God, knowing there is no more to do. (In my experience, I have found that the only action that is productive is *inspired* action.)

Finally

When I see clients, I am often their last resort or close to it. Most people try the allopathic Western approach before resorting to the less-accepted and scientifically unproven methods that I use. Clients often begin a session with me by saying, "I know this sounds crazy, but . . . ," and then they tell me their story.

I can assure them that they are not crazy. Knowing that there are many people who are afraid to be honest because they think themselves to be crazy or fear being judged by others distresses me. For that reason, I decided to share all of my own crazy stories to let people with this fear know that they are not alone. Once we are open to the possibilities of something existing beyond our comprehension of "normal," we can find a way to deal with it.

My hope in sharing my personal experiences is to help spread the word that there is much more than what we experience with our physical senses. Many people know and accept this as truth. Perhaps with this book, a few more eyes and minds will be open to these ideas.

If you have been dealing with an issue that has no logical answer, then perhaps the solution will come out of left field. That's where I find many of my answers.

Afterword

The Next to the Last Word . . .
Mechanism of Action Unknown
by Teri D'Andria, BA, MSOM, DAOM

I hope that for many of you who have stretched your minds or who have at least considered the possibilities of a more expanded point of view of energy healing, this is not the end of the trail for you. You might find it helpful to continue your explorations via the resources presented on Hoberleigh's SuperQuack website as well as engage in open dialogue on her blog.

For those readers who are still on the fence and whose worldviews remain firmly ensconced in the material domain, let's revisit the story of the engineer from the beginning of this book. Remember? He was one of Hoberleigh's clients, and he asked questions about what was happening behind his apparent improvements. Recall that these questions came during his third visit, and he was feeling better. But when Hoberleigh was unable to give him a mechanism of action, he stopped his sessions and never returned. If he couldn't get a handle on how the therapy was working, he chose not to continue.

Not knowing a precise mechanism of action has not stopped conventional therapies from being used. Let's consider pharmacology as an example. We have drugs that were part of conventional, standard care for years before we understood precisely how they worked, and some drugs' workings remain unknown today. Aspirin and anesthesia are two examples. Both of these agents were in wide use well before a precise mechanism of action was known, but not knowing how they worked did not preclude their use. No one in his or her right mind would elect to have surgery without anesthesia simply on the grounds that conventional medical research has not established its mechanism of action. It does the job, and it is fairly safe, and that suffices.

Most of what we know in the day-to-day world comes to us secondhand. As Hoberleigh pointed out, she doesn't know how a variety of things work, yet she uses them with confidence because somebody knew enough to develop them in the first place. Hoberleigh might have been able to tell this engineer some of the ideas behind what she does, but I imagine he would have had a hard time grasping the concepts. To him, it would be secondhand knowledge, further complicated by the fact that much of the practitioner's knowledge comes via apprehensions that are in a different domain than his knowledge of engineering. In other words, she would have been hard-pressed to frame her response in empirical, scientific terms. In that case, there was only one appropriate response she could have given him.

If he wanted a complete understanding of the kinds of experiential data with which the practitioner does her work, he would have to engage himself in spiritual study and practice. That is his answer. There is no other way. And notice that that was the case for the practitioner herself. There was only so far she could go rationally and mentally in reading about, studying, and hearing about energy healing. What she had to do, and ended up doing, was actually engaging in spiritual healing practice.

Fortunately for her, she had acquired a spiritual belief system that underpinned and drove her quest for understanding, and through actual spiritual practice, she learned that Spirit is not located out in left field or in right field or in center field. Spirit is the entire stadium, infinite in all directions, upon which the game is displayed; it is the field of all the fields, the player of all the players, the spectator of all the spectators, including all and transcending all.

So we are left with an invitation—an invitation to continue the quest. Energy healing has a legion of critics; the jury is still out. If there is only one more imperative to keep the horizon open for further research, it would be this: anything that has any potential at all to ease human pain and suffering deserves to have a place at the table. That alone justifies continued exploration into the field of energy healing.

Glossary

applied kinesiology: Also known as "muscle testing," this is considered by many to be a pseudoscientific system of muscle testing. I use it to gather information from somewhere other than the mind of the client. The client extends the arm straight out, parallel to the floor (or, when lying down, parallel to the wall), as I apply pressure near the wrist to push the arm down. I ask a yes-or-no question, and if the arm locks, the answer is no. If I am able to push the arm down, the answer is yes. Using this method while the subject holds substances can help me determine if an individual has a sensitivity to that substance.

BodyTalk: A modality founded by Dr. John Veltheim. This is the overview given by the website www.bodytalksystem.com:

> BodyTalk is an astonishingly simple and effective holistic therapy that allows the body's energy systems to be re-synchronized so they can operate as nature intended. Each system, cell, and atom is in constant communication with each other at all times. Through exposure to the stresses of day-to-day life, however, these lines of communication can become compromised or disconnected, which then leads to a decline in physical, emotional and/or mental well-being. Reconnecting these lines of communication enables the body's internal mechanisms to function at optimal levels, thus repairing and preventing disease

while rapidly accelerating the healing process. In this way, BodyTalk stimulates the body's innate ability to balance and heal itself on all levels.

chakra: A chakra is a funnel-shaped, spinning vortex of energy emanating from the body. Some say there are seven major chakras located on the midline of the body. Other systems include more. It is said that every acupuncture point is located on a major chakra, minor chakra, or minichakra.

cord cutting: This is the process of releasing an energetic bond located on a chakra (often the emotional solar-plexus chakra) that was established through an emotional connection with a person, place, or thing.

The Disappearance of the Universe: Straight Talk about Illusions, Past Lives, Religion, Sex, Politics, and the Miracles of Forgiveness: by Gary R. Renard, www.garyrenard.com. The book that helped me to understand *A Course in Miracles* and expand my perception of what happens beyond this 3-D illusion.

Emotional Freedom Techniques (EFT): Founded by Gary Craig, this is a modality one can use by oneself to release emotional disturbances by tapping on specific acupoints while focusing on an issue. A clear and thorough tutorial is located on the website www. emofree.com, and it is free.

forgiveness: Forgiveness is the choice to let go of a past hurt in order to free oneself from continued pain.

Genome Healing: www.genomehealing.com.au. Genome Healing is a technique taught by founder Carol Roberts, that teaches students to reprogram their DNA, and activate new blueprints for optimal functioning within organs and systems in the body.

Jaffee Mellor Technique (JMT): www.jmttechnique.com. This bioenergetic healing technique, founded by Carolyn Jaffe, D.Ac., Ph.D and Judy Mellor, RN, Ph.D., treats autoimmune diseases, asthma, allergies, chronic fatigue syndrome and many other disorders, using applied kinesiology, desensitization, deactivation and acupressure.

Joseph Murphy (1898-1981): He was a writer, teacher, lecturer, and minister-director of the Church of Divine Science, as well as author of over thirty books, including *The Power of Your Subconscious Mind*.

Matrix Energetics: www.matrixenergetics.com. Developed by Richard Bartlett D.C., N.D., this modality is described on the website as "a pathway to transformation. This transformation takes place by communicating at the quantum level with the wave fronts (energy and information) that create all of reality."

metaphysics: This is the branch of philosophy that deals with first causes. I think of it as that which is beyond the physical world.

muscle testing: See applied kinesiology.

Nambudripad's Allergy Elimination Technique (NAET): According to the overview from the website www.naet.com,

> NAET® was discovered by Dr. Devi S. Nambudripad in November of 1983. Nambudripad's Allergy Elimination Techniques, also known as NAET, are a non-invasive, drug free, natural solution to alleviate allergies of all types and intensities using a blend of selective energy balancing, testing and treatment procedures from acupuncture/ acupressure, allopathy, chiropractic, nutritional, and kinesiological disciplines of medicine.

Neuro-Emotional Technique (NET): According to the website link www.netmindbody.com/for-patients/an-explanation-of-net,

> NET Practitioners are nearly unlimited in their ability to address the physical and behavioral stress-related conditions of their patients. These conditions include headaches, body pains, phobias, general anxiety, self-sabotaging behaviors, organ dysfunctions and so much more. It's important to note that NET does not cure or heal the patient, but rather, NET removes blocks to the natural vitalism of the body, "allowing" the body to repair itself naturally.

Pranic Healing: According to the website www.pranichealing.com,

> Pranic Healing is a highly evolved and tested system of energy medicine developed by GrandMaster Choa Kok Sui that utilizes *prana* to balance, harmonize and transform the body's energy processes. *Prana* is a Sanskrit word that means *life-force*. This invisible bio-energy or vital energy keeps the body alive and maintains a state of good health. In acupuncture, the Chinese refer to this subtle energy as *Chi*. It is also called *Ruach* or the *Breath of Life* in Hebrew.

Quantum Touch: www.quantumtouch.com. This is a method of directing Life Force Energy to promote healing and optimal wellness throughout the body. Richard Gordon is the founder of this modality.

Reiki: An overview according to the website www.reiki.org is as follows:

> Reiki is a Japanese technique for stress reduction and relaxation that also promotes healing. It is administered by "laying on hands" and is based on the idea that an

unseen "life force energy" flows through us and is what causes us to be alive. If one's "life force energy" is low, then we are more likely to get sick or feel stress, and if it is high, we are more capable of being happy and healthy. The word Reiki is made of two Japanese words—Rei which means "God's Wisdom or the Higher Power" and Ki which is "life force energy". So Reiki is actually "spiritually guided life force energy."

Reiki attunements: According to www.reiki.org,

Reiki is not taught in the way other healing techniques are taught. It is transferred to the student by the Reiki Master during an attunement process. This process opens the crown, heart, and palm chakras and creates a special link between the student and the Reiki source.

Religious Science: According to the textbook *The Science of Mind* by Ernest Holmes, "Religious Science is a correlation of laws of science, opinions of philosophy, and revelations of religion applied to human needs and the aspirations of man." The Church of Religious Science now goes by the name Centers for Spiritual Living.

Religious Science practitioner: One who is trained to practice affirmative prayer known as a treatment.

Science of Mind: The teachings and textbook by Ernest Holmes, which are what the Church of Religious Science (now Centers for Spiritual Living) is based upon. The teachings explain the laws of the universe in regard to manifestation.

solar-plexus chakra: Energy vortex located on the midline of the front of the body in the hollow just below the breastbone. It is considered the seat of emotions and, on a physiological level, is associated with many of the digestive organs.

surrogate: During muscle testing, a surrogate is someone who stands in for the client when he or she is unable to be tested directly.

test: Whenever I say, "I tested . . . ," I am referring to muscle testing, or applied kinesiology. I am only able to confirm a yes or no answer using this method or a sensitivity to a substance.

theta: This is a deep state of relaxation common to hypnosis. Brain waves in this state have a frequency of four to seven cycles per second. To compare, beta brain waves register at fourteen to twenty-eight cycles per second. This is an active and alert state. Alpha registers at seven to fourteen cycles per second. This is a relaxed and meditative state.

ThetaHealing: This is a method of healing founded by Vianna Stibal that teaches one how to attain a theta brain wave. According to the website www.thetahealing.com/about-thetahealing,

> In 1995 Vianna Stibal, a Naturopath, Massage Therapist, and Intuitive Reader at the time, discovered that the way she did readings could do an instant healing. Vianna . . . was diagnosed with cancer that was quickly destroying her right femur. Everything she had tried using conventional and alternative medicine had failed. Then she discovered that the simple technique she used in Readings could heal. Her leg was instantaneously healed . . . Vianna solicited the help of a physicist and with an electroencephalograph discovered that the simple technique tapped Theta waves. Over many years of practicing the technique, Vianna believes the technique utilizes a Theta wave to achieve an instant healing.

Acknowledgments

I am grateful to all of my teachers who have helped me along my path, beginning with my parents, who taught me to follow my inner wisdom rather than the ways of the world.

I also thank

all of my invisible guides, teachers, angels, and helpers whom I may or may not know about;

my visible angels, including Trisha Robere for her editing and surrogate skills, Dr. Theresa D'Andria for her wisdom in both left and right field, and her contributions to this book, Jeane Marie for her editorial contributions, Lauren Hinds for her creative suggestions and assistance with the cover design and for being an awesome surrogate for me, Amanda Sargenti, for her wonderful way with words, Carol Goans for support and insights, and Genie McAllister for encouragement along the way;

Michael Moore for introducing me to Religious Science;

all my Religious Science teachers, especially to the memory of Rev. Helen Street;

the members of my little "Algonquin group" (Durrell, Vivian, Dave, Maryl Jo, Joe, Sylvia, Greg, and Kevin) for constant inspiration and interesting discussions;

Dr. Moon, who opened my eyes to energy medicine and suggested that I study acupuncture;

all of my professors at Samra University of Oriental Medicine; and all of my teachers in energy medicine, including Dr. Devi Nambudripad, who taught me NAET; Drs. Scott and Deborah Walker for teaching me NET; the memory of Dr. John Thie for my classes in Touch for Health and for teaching me, whenever possible, to train with the best; Dr. Eric Pearl for giving me the best chiropractic adjustment of my life and teaching me the Reconnection; Drs. Carolyn Jaffee and Judy Mellor, who taught me JMT; Dr. John Veltheim, the founder of BodyTalk; Gary Craig, from whom I learned EFT; Charlie Blanchard, who taught me Quantum Touch; Dr. Richard Bartlett for teaching me Matrix Energetics; Alain Herriott, who taught me Core Transformation; Master Stephen Co, my teacher of Pranic Healing; Carol Roberts for teaching me Genome Healing; Vianna Stibal, the founder of ThetaHealing; and my teacher Marina Rose.

Thanks to Barbara McKell for permission to include her article on cord-cutting.

Thanks to my church, the Church of Truth–Center for Awakening Consciousness, especially Rev. Dr. Donna Byrns, for all the love and support I've received throughout the last few years.

I want to thank all those who have allowed me to work with them— or, as I prefer to say, to play with them—because of all I have learned during the process.

My heartfelt thanks to everyone whose story has ended up in this book. I cannot name you because of privacy issues, but if it weren't for you, this book would not exist.

And last, but not least, I want to thank my entire team at Balboa Press. I deeply appreciate all the help, support, and encouragement I received throughout this new endeavor of becoming an author.